# Prophecies
# Converging in Our Time

## John Van Auken

Includes the Last Pope, Nostradamus' timing and Antichrists, the Messages from Mary, the Mother of Jesus, the Egyptian timeline, the Seven Ages of Humanity, Physical Earth Changes, Prophecies in the Bible, and Edgar Cayce's Visions.

*Living in the Light*
Virginia Beach, Virginia USA

ISBN-13: 978-1981981731
ISBN-10: 198198173X


JohnVanAuken.com
JohnVanAuken.Newsletter@Gmail.com

Living in the Light
P.O. Box 4942
Virginia Beach VA 23454 USA

Other books by this author
are available from
Amazon.com
JohnVanAuken.com

John Van Auken is the Director of the
Edgar Cayce Foundation

# Prophecies Converging in Our Time

## CONTENTS

## A Guarantee...

*I guarantee the following prophecy will come true*: One year from reading these words you will not be the same person you are today, and your life and the life of those around you will have changed. This is an easy prophecy to make because life is *always* changing – *within* us and all *around* us.

That is a guarantee. I am not the one guaranteeing it, no; the great River of Life is making this guarantee. The Forces of Life *flow* on and on, ever changing, and catching all of us in its currents. No one is exempt.

Now the big question is: "Do you want the River of Life to determine how you will change or do *YOU* want to play a key role in determining the direction of the change?" "Are you the captain of your vessel on the river, the navigator of your journey, or simply a passenger?"

As helpless or self-determined as we may feel, we would be wise to become aware of the prophecies that saw the River of Life from a higher perspective and have shared that view with us.

### Predestination

From the moment that those famous words were spoken – "Let there be Light" – and the Big Bang exploded with life and light in the darkness, a direction was set, and life has been flying on that course ever since. Yet, in the midst of this set course there is a degree of free-will, of self-determination – but it has to work within the framework of set course. The freedom may only be in how we react to the flow of life, but there is a freedom in that. However, many believe that we do have more freedom than we realize.

How do we master the powerful currents of life's flow? How can we direct our vessel to a destination that *we desire?* Do we even know what we desire? These questions need to be answered even before we begin to master our course of our life on the great River.

Of course, we are not likely to *divert* the River of Life to our way of thinking but we may determine where in the river we sail or swim – how deep, how fast, amid what debris, and with what people, what wind do we catch in our sails and what wind do we "tack" against in order stay *our* course.

In order to do this we must have some idea of *from* where and *to* where the River of Life flows, and what are the various depths and characteristics within the River of Life and the winds. And where in this river are we *karmically* located? We must *know* the powerful currents in the water and when the wind are blowing favorably or unfavorably. We also have to *strengthen* ourselves, and *develop* our skills. We have to determine with what attitude, what emotions, and what principles will we live by in life's journey.

**Prophecy: Identifying the Flow of the Forces**

How can there be a *knowing* before an event occurs? How can any human or god see a future that has not occurred? The answer is found in our *origin* and how the future has already been determined by our origin – both as individuals and as a humanity, in the microcosm of self and the macrocosm of the Cosmos.

Science has studied the origins of the universe and there is much evidence indicating where it is going and how it will end. So we discover the same about ourselves, as individuals and as a collective group.

Who is our original self? I don't write "was" because that original self is still within us. There may be layers and layers of experiences on top of the original self, but deep inside us the original you and me remains.

Please don't tell me that you still think we are simply the result of sperm and egg, and the evolution of our material existence? If so, then we have roughly 80 to 100 years and then we are nothing – finished. The whole journey was just some years of entertainment, confusion, pain, and happiness leading to *nothing*.

Physical incarnation is only a portion of the story of humanity – as individuals and as a group. Ancient tales, classic philosophical reflections, and theological proclamations declare that humanity is more than cellular division and specialization to form a temporary physical being that leads to nothingness – and the incarnation is of no lasting value or purpose.

Throughout time and regardless of geography, culture, and religious beliefs humans have felt, have believed that there is more to humanity than physicality. And there is.

Bishop Malachy's Visions of 112 Popes!

# 1. The Last Pope

## Bishop Malachy's Vision of 112 Popes
*Pope Frances is the Last Pope!*
*Nostradamus'*

This legendary tale begins in 1139 when the Bishop of Ireland visited the Vatican to report on his diocese. His name was Malachy (pronouced *mal-ah-kee* or *mal-ah-ki*, as in "sky," also spelled Malachi). According to a book written in 1592, Malachy, while at the Vatican, fell into a deep trance during which he saw the next pontiff, Celestine II (1143-1144) and the *entire* line of successive of popes, all 112 of them; then he saw the destruction of the city of Rome. When the bishop awoke, he wrote a complete manuscript of the vision, giving each of the prophesied popes a Latin motto reflecting a key characteristic of their person or activity. The manuscript was misplaced or hidden in the archives of the Vatican for roughly 400 years. Now you might feel that losing a manuscript of this importance hard to believe but consider that there are roughly a million books plus some 75,000 historical codices (*ancient* manuscripts) in the Vatican Library.

There are critics of the authenticity of this legend and the manuscript associated with it. And since the original document has not been found and no recorded mention of it occurs prior to 1592, their criticism is worthy of noting here. First, if this is true, then why did Malachy's biographer and life-long friend, Bernard of Clairvaux, never mention the prophecy in his biography of Malachy or in his correspondence with the bishop?

The critics' second argument is about Arnold Wion, the Benedictine historian who first mentioned Malachy's document and prophecies in his 1592 book *Lignum Vitae* (English: *Tree of Life*). They presume that Wion simply made the story up? Personally, I find it difficult to believe that Wion created this whole story with all of its elaborate details and then attributed it to a 420-year-old bishop from Ireland. It would make more sense that Wion reported the story after hearing about it from some source in his time? But it's difficult to accept the he made the story up. More likely the legend had traveled via word-of-mouth to Wion's hearing. However, if Wion did in deed make the story up, then he is certainly the prophet, for much of the information about the future popes – 425 years beyond Wion – is quite accurate.

The counter to this criticism is that Wion once lived in France at the very Abbey that Malachy's biographer and friend Bernard of Clairvaux founded! There he may have actually seen or been told details of Malachy's manuscript titled, *Prophetia S. Malachiae, Archiepiscopi, Summis Pontificibus* (English: *Prophecy of St. Malachi, and the Archbishops, the Supreme Pontiffs*). Add to this that Malachy actually died at the Abbey of Clairvaux, causing some to speculate that Malachy may have actually had his manuscript with him at the Abbey of Clairvaux.

Furthermore, the story that Malachy left the document with the pope in the Vatican did not appear until 1871! In 1871 in the *Journal de Saone-et-Loire*, Abbé Cucherat published an article about Malachy's manuscript and stated that Malachy left the document with Pope Innocent II (1130-1143) as a "comfort" to him during troubling times for the Church. You see, Innocent's election was controversial, a majority of cardinals did not accept his election. Thus, his reign was marked by a struggle for recognition against the supporters of Antipope Anacletus II. (There have been some 40 antipopes in the Roman Catholic Church's history – a person claiming to be pope while a duly elected Pope was still in office.) At one point Innocent had to flee from Rome to France. There France's Louis VI decided that Innocent was the legitimate pope. After two more attempts to regain his rightful place in the Holy See in Rome, Innocent finally took control and ended the schism in 1139. It helped that Anacletus died. 1139 was the same year that Malachy arrived in the Vatican to report to the pope, that being Innocent II. However, Malachy may not have left his manuscript with the pope, and when he died it remained in the Abbey of Clairvaux, later to be seen by Wion. What happened to it after that is unknown.

We have to pause and wonder how could 112 popes be known *before* they were chosen by vote. Is the fate of humanity so clearly known at some unseen level of consciousness and life? Are we living out some drama that has *already occurred* in some other dimension, and is now being repeated on a material stage with each actor playing their part according to prewritten scripts and predesigned sets? Was William Shakespeare correct when he wrote in *As You Like It* (Act II, Scene VII): "All the world's a stage, And all the men and women merely players; They have their exits and their entrances, And one man/woman in his/her time plays many parts."

Can someone know the future by simply looking ahead in the story of humanity?

Whatever the answer may be, the Bishop of Ireland's vision has been surprisingly accurate! Seeing in 1139 Malachy foresaw our 20th Century popes and gave them Latin mottos that described them, some perfectly and some oddly! Let's briefly review them.

## Pius X

Malachy called Pius X "Ignis ardens," meaning

*Ardent Fire.* So ardent was his faith and teachings that he was canonized a saint in 1954. Pius X encouraged everyone to live a holy life and to have daily practices that strengthen their piety. He encouraged receiving communion frequently to imbue one's body and mind with the Holy Spirit. He raised the holiness of Jesus' mother Mary in the Church, being himself deeply devoted to Mary, and granting official devotional titles and decrees of her around the world, and stating that there was no surer way to Christ than through his Holy Mother. This may have been a catalyst for the many Apparitions of Mary in the 20th Century, including the coming Fatima apparitions and their prophecies in 1917.

## Benedict XV

Malachy saw Benedict XV, 1914 to 1922, and called him "Religio Depopulata," which relates to him being the pope during World War I (1914-1918), the "War to End all Wars!" The total number of civilian and military casualties in WWI is estimated at around 37 million people! And this war was precipitated the secularization of religion in Europe and Russia. This was certainly a period of "depopulation of religion."

## Pius XI

Pius XI (1922-1939) received the Malachy motto "Fides intrepida," meaning *Fearless Faith*, likely referring to his stand against Fascism and Communism that were a rising force against the Church, ultimately leading to World War II (1939-1945). He was the first ruler of the independent state of Vatican City, established in 1929. He boldly challenged Nazi Germany with a Papal encyclical called *On the Church and the German Reich*, with the first words, *Mit brennender Sorge*, "With Burning Concern." He did not write this in Latin but in German, and he had it smuggled into Germany for fear of censorship and read from the pulpits of all German Catholic churches! Fearless Faith fits him well.

## Pius XII

Malachy then saw Pius XII, 1939 to 1958, and called him "Pastor Angelicus," possibly referring to his angelic shepherding of the Church against the Nazi rise to power and Nazi anti-Semitic and anti-Catholic aggressions. However, some critics feel that Pius' relationship with Mussolini and Fascism was too cooperative. However, Pius did raise strong resistance when Mussolini established anti-Jewish laws in 1938 prohibiting marriages between Jews and non-Jews, including Catholics. The Vatican viewed this as a violation of the 1929 Latern Concordat that gave the church the sole right to regulate marriages involving Catholics. These were trying times for spirituality and the Church. It's difficult to fit this motto with this man. However, the angelic portion of his motto may refer to his mystical experiences, many reported that this pope saw visions.

## John XXIII

Pius XII was then followed by John XXIII, 1958-63, called "Pastor et Nauta" (meaning *shepherd and navigator*), likely referring to his position as Archbishop of Venice, a city on an island in shallow Venetian Lagoon. The "shepherd" portion of his motto may refer to his reconvening of the Ecumenical Council for the first time since 1869, because the Council used the symbols of a *cross and a ship* – indicative of the Shepherd and Navigator. This motto appears to fit well.

## Paul VI

After John XXIII came Malachy's "Flos Florum" (*Flower of Flowers*), Paul VI (1963-78) whose coat of arms contained a floral design with three lilies. He sought  numerous reforms and reached out with a "floral" attitude that fostered improved relations with the Eastern Orthodox Church and even with Protestants. This resulted in many historic meetings and agreements. Again, this motto appears to fit.

John Paul I

But here comes the most shocking and surprising of Malachy's insights! After Paul VI came a short reign for Malachy's "De Mediatate Lunae" (*the middle or half of the moon*) – John Paul I (August 26 to September 28, 1978). This is one of the shortest and most suspicious papal reigns. Apparently, 839 years before it occured, Malachy saw how short this pope's reign would be.

And when it comes to John Paul I, Nostradamus had visions into what may actually have happened to John Paul I. Here's what Nostradamus saw and wrote in his poetic quatrains:

He who will have government of the Great Cape
Will be led to take action
The twelve Red Ones will come to spoil the cover
Under murder, murder will come to be done.
(Century 4, Quatrain 11)

Hidden in these words are visions of the papacy that Nostradamus wanted to hide from the Inquisition in fear for his life and the lives of those close to him. But today we may have the advantage of history on our side in interpreting this quatrain. First, "the Great Cape" is very likely the Pope. Over his cassock the Pope will wear a lace *rochet*. Over the rochet is worn the red Papal *mozzetta*, a shoulder cape that has a collar and is buttoned all the way down the front. In the most formal of events covers all of this with a truly great cape called the *mantum*.

"Led to take action" may very well be John Paul I's three deadly decisions: (1) investigate the Vatican Bank for laundering Mafia money, (2) to meet with a delegation of women to discuss a greater role for women in the Church, and (3) seek out priests who have secret and forbidden memberships in clandestine organizations. These secret organizations would include the Freemasons, Illuminati, Carbonari, Odd-Fellows, Knights of Pythias, Sons of Temperance, and several more. If discovered, these priests – and I suspect several higher ranking church authorities – would be openly charged with violating Church law. It was long believed that these secret organizations conspired against the Church, even in some cases against the State.

Nostradamus' "Twelve Red Ones" is easy: they are the Cardinals, all of whom wear scarlet red cassocks and mozzettas. These Red Ones will spoil the elected pope's cover of protection. There are now over 200 cardinals but only a few are close advisors to the pope. Apparently, Nostradamus saw twelve were involved in the quick elimination of John Paul I.

The final line, "under murder, murder will come to be done," could be a reference to the first murder by poison and the second being in the violation of papal death customs through cremation.

Nostradamus also saw poison:

When the sepulcher of the great Roman is found
The day after will be elected a Pope
By his Senate he will not be approved
Poisoned is his blood by the sacred chalice. (3:65)

When Pope Paul VI was laid in his "sepulcher" and the new pope was chosen by the "Senate" of Cardinals, John Paul I offended the Cardinals with his three controversial decisions that would have shined a dark light on the Church. Some believe that since John Paul I only lasted in office for 33 days, he was poisoned for these decisions – of course it was with the best of intentions to preserve the honor of the Church! This rationalization is often used when doing evil for good purposes.

John Paul I was only 66 and in good health when he suddenly died. He had disturbed his Curia (Senate of Cardinals) by stating in one of his earliest speeches that God was not only the Heavenly Father but also the Heavenly Mother. He expressed openly his support of women's rights and agreed to meet with a U.S. Congressional delegation to discuss artificial birth control! But his most fatal directive came when he asked his Secretary of State, Cardinal Jean Villot, to begin an investigation of the Vatican Bank for laundering Mafia money, and to identify priests who had secret memberships in the Freemason's Lodge P2. The next morning he was dead. Roman police investigators were surprised that Cardinal Villot initially gave them false information during their questioning and that they quickly embalmed the Pope's body, then cremated it before any autopsy could be done to determine the cause of death. Stranger still, Cardinal Villot died within six months after these events and the nun Sister Vincenza Taffarel, who found the body and was a key witness to events surrounding the body, was sent into isolation and could no longer be reached by police investigators.

In 1978 the Chicago Tribune published an article titled, "Evidence of foul play in Pope death claimed." (October 7, 1978). In 1984 David Yallop published his book titled, *In God's Name*, detailing the conspiracy. The 1990 motion picture *The Godfather Part III* featured an element of the story involving organized crime during and after the death of the old pope. In 2003 Daniel Silva published his book titled, "The Confessor," in which the Soviet Union plotted with Cardinal Jean Villot to assassinate John Paul I. In 2014 Colombian writer Evelio Rosero published a book on the pope's death, *El papa envenenado* ("The Poisoned Pope").

### John Paul II

After John Paul I, Malachy saw a pope that he nicknamed, "De Labore Solis" (*the labor of the sun*), John Paul II, Karol Wojtyla from Poland. Again it appears that Malachy's motto was accurate.

Here's where the famous seer Nostradamus enters our research, for some of Nostradamus' quatrains appear to "see" John Paul II's hardships.

Author and researcher J.H. Brennan pointed out that the part of Poland from which John Paul II came was originally a portion of ancient France, and therefore the following quatrain may refer to him:

Not from Spain, but from *ancient* France
He will be elected from the trembling ship
To the enemy he will make assurance
Who in his reign will be a cruel blight (5:49)

Brennan, considers the "trembling ship" to be the Christian Church itself, which had lost its role in Russia during the Bolshevik Revolution in "Red October," 25 October 1917 (Old Style dating, 7 November New Style). This revolution created the world's first atheist state. Nostradamus' "enemy" would be none other than the Soviet Union against Polish labor union supporter John Paul II. As pope he made "assurances" (line 3) to the Soviets concerning the strikes in Poland by the workers; assurances that may have kept the Soviets from doing what they had done to other countries. It is said that John Paul II sent a message to Moscow that if they mounted an invasion against Poland, as they had done in Hungary and Czechoslovakia, he would fly to Warsaw and stand in full papal regalia before the approaching tanks. Brennan goes on to say that though John Paul II was successful in this situation, the Soviet "cruel blight" (line 4) continued through much of his early years as pope.

Then came the Soviet assassination attempt. Poland's Solidarity movement (the first independent labor union in a Soviet-bloc country) was seen as the most significant threat to Soviet power in Eastern Europe. It was believed that the KGB was behind the shooting of John Paul II. Mehmet Ali Agca was the Turk who shot John Paul in St. Peter's Square. John Paul recounted that he was riding through the Square (13 May 1981) when he saw a young girl wearing an Our Lady of Fatima medallion (the date of the first Apparition of Mary in Fatima was 13 May 1917, so the day of the shooting was an anniversary date). John Paul stopped the vehicle and reached down to bless the medallion at the same moment that Agca fired a 9mm Browning Hi-Power semi-automatic pistol, hitting the pope 4 times, severely wounding him, but not killing him. John Paul told the doctors to give him the bullets. and he then took the bullets to Fatima, Portugal, and placed them in the crown of the Our Lady of Fatima statue. (We'll review the Fatima Prophecies later.)

But it was the *second* assassination attempt on John Paul II that caught Nostradamus' attention:

Oh great Rome, your ruin comes close
Not of your walls, but of your blood and substance
The sharp one of letters will be so horrible a notch
Pointed steel placed up his sleeve, ready to wound. (10:65)

In this attempt the stabber was an educated but ultra-conservative priest. His name was Juan Fernandez Krohn. He was considered to be an expert in art and literature, thus a "sharp one of letters." During the pope's visit to Portugal in 12-13 May 1982, Krohn pulled a long knife from out of his sleeve ("pointed steel placed up his sleeve") and attempted to kill John Paul II. The pope was wounded and bleeding ("of your blood and substance") by the knife-wielding priest on the eve of the first Fatima apparition and one year after he had been shot in St Peter's Square. The event was recounted several years later by the pope's secretary: On 12 May 1982, the pope was visiting the shrine city of Fatima in Portugal to give thanks for surviving the first assassination attempt. Krohn, an ultra-conservative Spanish priest, lunged at the pope with a dagger, cutting him, and then was knocked to the ground by police and arrested.

Later, Krohn explained that he was opposed to the reforms of Vatican II and believed Pope John Paul II was working *with* the Soviet Union against the Church, and was secretly a Communist agent trying to corrupt the Vatican! This assassination attempt did not receive any press because the pope, his secretary, and his supporters (including the police) kept it a secret. But Nostradamus certainly seems to have viewed this event some 430 years *before* it occurred, even noting the failure, "your ruin comes close." The attempted assassination was *close* to being a success.

Despite these attempted assassination attempts, John Paul II's reign was the second longest in recorded history – 26 years, 5 months and 18 days.

### Benedict XVI

After Pope John Paul II, Malachy predicted only two more popes will reign, after which the Church will be dramatically changed.

In April of 2005 German Cardinal Joseph Aloisius Ratzinger was elected pope. At the time he was the oldest cardinal ever to be elected pope, 78. He took the name Benedict XVI. At first glance this name does not appear to be in line with Malachy's vision! Malachy gave the Latin motto, *Gloria Olivae* (glory of the olive) to this pope. Many were briefly confused, including me. I thought for sure that the Archbishop of Paris, Cardinal Jean-Marie Lustiger, was to become the "Glory of the Olive" in Malachy's accurate line. That's because the olive has long been a sign for the Jews (a dove brought Noah an olive leaf after the great flood), and Cardinal Lustiger was born a Jew of two Jewish parents – thus, the glory of the olive would be a converted Jew! Made a lot of sense at the time, not only to me but to many others. However, a German cardinal was elected and took the name Benedict. It wasn't until researchers realized and reported that the Benedictines are known as the *Olivetans!* Only then did everyone realize how accurate Malachy was! And one of the major Abbeys of the Benedictines is at the foot of the Mt. of Olives. Of course the highest ranking among the Benedictines would be "the glory" of the Olivetans.

We should note here that as a cardinal and as a pope few higher-ups in the Church aggressively pursued the prosecution and expulsion of priests involved in sexual child abuse than Ratziner/Benedict. And during his time as a cardinal he was often thwarted in his efforts by higher powers in the Vatican. He insisted that the Church follow civil law about such crimes, often referring to it as "filth in the Church."

Benedict resigned his papacy because of age and ill health in 2013.

### The Last Pope – Francis

Now comes the last pope in the 112 list that Malachy envisioned so long ago. He gave this last pope the Latin motto: *Petrus Romanus,* meaning "Peter the Roman." Born Jorge Mario Bergoglio in Argentina, he was elected pope in 2013 at the age of 76, and continues to reign as of this writing. When he took the name Francis, many felt it did not fit with Malachy's motto of Peter the Roman.

Nevertheless, there has been much conjecture about how Pope Francis may actually fit the prophecy's *Petrus Romanus*. For example, Cardinal Bergoglio took the name "Francis" in honor of St. Francis of Assisi, and this is where the motto may find its place in the prophecy's list. Let's take a brief look at St. Francis of Assisi.

The saint was one of several children by Italian fabric merchant Pietro (Peter) di Bernardone and his wife Pica de Bourlemont, a French noblewoman originally from Provence, France. The father was in France on business when Francis was born in Assisi, and Pica had him baptized as Giovanni (John) di Pietro (Peter) di Bernardone. Upon the father's return to Assisi, he called his son *Francesco* ("the Frenchman"), Francesco di Pietro di Bernardone. Now some writers state that Pietro di Bernardone can be translated, "Peter the Roman," saying that Bernardone was part of the Roman Empire, and was somehow associated with Assisi. Assisi was in fact a part of the *Sexta Regio* ("6th Region") of the 11 regions into which the Roman emperor Augustus divided the nation. Today the region is called Roman Umbria, or simply Umbria. When the Western portion of the Roman Empire fell in September 476, that included Assisi and some say Bernardone.

Additionally, some writers take Pope Francis' natural last name, *Bergoglio,* and break it into its parts: *berg* means "mountain" and *oglio* means "oil" to refer to Assisi, which has *Rocca Maggiore*, literally "Big Rock," a fortress in Assisi. And then they jump to the association of "the Rock" to the name "Peter" and Jesus' statement: "Thou art Peter, and upon this rock I will build my church." (Matthew 16:18) One could interpret Malachy's vision as having seen Pietro (Peter) di Bernardone as part of the Roman Empire and with the name Peter. Thus, we get to Petrus Romanus, Peter the Roman. It is certainly not an easy fit with Malachy's motto.

### The Destruction of the City

Here are the last words of Malachy's prophecy:

In Latin: *In persecutione extrema S.R.E. sedebit.Petrus Romanus, qui pascet oves in multis tribulationibus, quibus transactis civitas septicollis diruetur, & judex tremendus judicabit populum suum. Finis.*

In English: "In the final persecution of the Holy Roman Church, there will sit Peter the Roman, who will pasture his sheep in many tribulations, and when these things are finished, the city of seven hills will be destroyed, and the dreadful judge will judge his people. The End."

The seven hills of Rome are Aventine, Caelian, Capitoline, Esquiline, Palatine, Quirinal, and Viminal. And the Servian Walls were constructed to protect the seven hills.

Malachy's "many tribulations" could refer to Pope Francis' challenges with sexual child abuse by priests, growing homosexuality, birth control, divorce, a greater role for women in the Church, priests being allowed to marry, Islamic terrorism and threats against the Church, and continuing growth of secularism. All these difficult issues are adding to the worldwide demand that the Roman Catholic Church resolve these issues or at least address them in some understandable manner.

Now let's consider how Rome could be destroyed after Pope Francis' reign. This may well be a result of *natural forces* from Italy's seismic faults and volcanoes. If fact, Italy has one of only six super-volcanoes on our planet. Here's a National Geographic (Dec. 22, 2016) report:

"A long-quiet yet huge super-volcano that lies under 500,000 people in Italy may be waking up and approaching a 'critical state,' scientists reported this week in the journal *Nature Communications.*

"Based on physical measurements and computer modeling: 'We propose that magma could be approaching the CDP [critical degassing pressure] at Campi Flegrei, a volcano in the metropolitan area of Naples, one of the most densely inhabited areas in the world, and where accelerating deformation and heating are currently being observed,' wrote the scientists – who are led by Giovanni Chiodini of the Italian National Institute of Geophysics in Rome."

Like other super-volcanoes – such as the one responsible for the geothermal activities in Yellowstone National Park – it is not a single volcanic *cone.* Rather, it's a large complex, much of it underground causing geysers and vents to release hot gas.

Five miles east of Naples is Mt. Vesuvius, best known for its eruption in AD 79 which led to the burying and destruction of the Roman city of Pompeii. Vesuvius is part of the so-called Campanian Volcanic Arc around the bay of Naples. The Arc includes Campi Flegrei, Mt. Vesuvius, Mt. Epomeo, Palinuro, Vavilev, Marsili, and Magnaghi. Further south are the active volcanoes Stromboli and Vulcano, and the very active Mt. Etna on Sicily. In addition to these there is a major fault line running down the eastern coast of Italy, and crossing over the southern portion of the country. Any of these seismic faults could cause massive destruction. Would any of these be what St. Malachy saw in his vision? Possibly. A super-volcano like Campi Flegrei would cause massive destruction, not only to Italy but to all nearby countries and the planet's atmosphere.

We don't just have Malachy's vision of destruction to Rome. The prophecies given at the Church-recognized apparition of Mother Mary at Fatima,

Portugal, in 1917 also predict destruction, and with images which are very volcanic! There were three messages given to the children at Fatima. Here's the first one that seems to reveal the fires of a volcano.

The First Message of Fatima:

"Our Lady showed us [Lúcia Santos (9 years old) and her cousins Jacinta (6) and Francisco Marto (8)] a great sea of fire which seemed to be under the earth. Plunged in this fire were demons and souls in human form, like transparent burning embers, all blackened or burnished bronze, floating about in the conflagration [obviously an adult wrote their verbal testimony using adult words], now raised into the air by the flames that issued from within themselves together with great clouds of smoke, now falling back on every side like sparks in a huge fire, without weight or equilibrium, and amid shrieks and groans of pain and despair, which horrified us and made us tremble with fear."

A "fire under the earth" sure sounds like magma, and "raised into the air ... with great clouds of smoke" sounds like a volcanic eruption.

The Third Message of Fatima:

In the Third message of Fatima the children see a ruined city and the pope. Here's the third message of Fatima as remembered and verbally retold to a bishop by Lucia, and subsequently recorded in writing.

"We [Lúcia Santos and her cousins Jacinta and Francisco Marto] saw in an immense light that is God: 'something similar to how people appear in a mirror when they pass in front of it,' a Bishop dressed in White 'we had the impression that it was the Holy Father' [pope]. Other Bishops, Priests, men and women Religious going up a steep mountain, at the top of which there was a big Cross of rough-hewn trunks as of a cork-tree with the bark [Oak]; before reaching there the Holy Father passed through a big city half in ruins, and half trembling with halting step, afflicted with pain and sorrow, he prayed for the souls of the corpses he met on his way; having reached the top of the mountain, on his knees at the foot of the big Cross he was killed by a group of soldiers who fired bullets and arrows at him, and in the same way there died one after another the other Bishops, Priests, men and women Religious, and various lay people of different ranks and positions. Beneath the two arms of the Cross there were two Angels each with a crystal aspersorium [a handheld implement used to sprinkle holy water] in his hand, in which they gathered up the blood of the Martyrs and with it sprinkled the souls that were making their way to God."

In this recounting of the vision, Lucia sees a "big city half in ruin," presumed to be Rome. She sees the pope killed by "bullets and arrows" from "soldiers." Some believe these soldiers may be ISIS sympathizers carrying out their threat to assassinate the pope and kill Christians. Today, it is difficult to see any "soldiers" other than Islamic terrorists that would attack the Vatican in our times. However, the 1917 vision may have been about the potential dangers of such an event throughout World War I (1914-1918) and World War II (1939-1945) when many soldiers could have entered the Vatican. Why "arrows"? Is this just a child's vision of weaponry? Could it be a symbol? And if it is a symbol, then could all the other elements of this vision be symbolic? If it were a dream, how might one interpret it? Could the pope and the other religious people have been seen struggling with climbing the mountain of problems they faced, as Malachy saw with his "many tribulations" for the pope? Could the bullets and arrows be recent sins (bullets) and old sins (arrows) karmically attacking the papacy and religious leaders, even lay Christians? Could the great tree and cross symbolize the ancient metaphor of the Tree of Life that is found in the legends and tales of most all ancient mythologies – connecting Heaven and the Underworld through our world? Tree-of-Life symbolism is found in Hinduism, Persian Zoroastrianism, Judaism, Kabbalah, Buddhism, Taoism, Norse mythology, the mythology of Maya, Aztec, Izapan, Mixtec, and Olmec peoples, even Islam and modern Mormonism. The Tree of Life is mentioned in the first book of the Bible (Genesis 3:22-24). A cross is seen as the Tree of Death, and it was believed that only through the crucifixion of one's desires and egotistical urges may one regain access to the Tree of Life, lost to humanity during the fall from grace in the original Garden of Eden, the paradise of God's company.

Whatever the correct understanding of the third prophecy of Fatima may be, it is clear that the Church and its leadership, along with a big city, are going to experience painful change. And Malachy saw that change coming fully with the 112th pope in his vision, Francis I, the last pope.

## 2. The Timing of World Change

### Nostradamus' Visions
#### (1503-1566 A.D.)

In the year 1555, Michel de Nostradame published the first edition of his prophetic book series entitled *Centuries*. He was already a well-known author, having published an annual almanac since 1550, and was famed for his cure for the Black Death (plague) of the Middle Ages. However famous he was in his lifetime, it did not compare to the fame he has gained since his death.

Now he is known throughout the world as "Nostradamus," a prophet who saw so many events in the future, many of them occurring in our times, that we have to consider his visions in our study of converging prophecies.

Nostradamus was born to Jewish parents in a Europe under the cruel, suspicious gaze of the Inquisition. His parents raised him Roman Catholic; but converted Jews were highly suspect in the eyes of the Inquisitor. And although he was a doctor, trained at the best medical school of his time, he was not readily accepted by his peers. These were the days when medicine was dominated by the practice of blood-letting with leeches, which Nostradamus openly refused to do, choosing to treat with clean drinking water, clean bathing water, clean garments and bedding, herbs and rose hip pills of his own making, which were as popular then as our vitamin-C pills are today. When you combine his questionable religious legitimacy and his questionable medical practices with his prophesying, he was in very grave danger of the fear and suspicion of the people of his time. Nostradamus once wrote, "Here where I reside, I carry on my work among animals, barbarians, mortal enemies of learning and letters." If it were not for his success with curing plague victims and prophesying accurately for the Royal families in secular power, he probably would have died at the burning stake of the Inquisition. When you consider that he was most certainly practicing an ancient, and mostly pagan, method of divination in order to receive his visions, he was, according to the Inquisition's list of evils, a perfect example of the evil that "must be purged from our presence." Fortunately, they never quite got their hands on him. He died, as he prophesied, on July 2, 1566 in the exact position and manner that he had foreseen.

In the beginning of his *Century* series he describes his method as follows:

Seated alone in secret study
Alone it rests on the brazen tripod
A slender flame licks out of the solitude
Making possible that which would have been in vain.
(Century 1, quatrain 1)

The wand in his hand is placed between the branches
He moistens the hem of his garment and his foot
Fear arises and a voice sets him trembling in his robes
In divine splendor, a god sits nearby. (1:2)

Anyone familiar with the manuscripts *De Mysteriis Egyptorum* by Iamblichus, *De Demonibus* by Michael Psellus and the legendary *The Key of Solomon*, all forbidden by the Inquisition, would know that these two quatrains reveal a knowledge of the specific methods used in these manuscripts for the evocation of spirits. To be in possession of one of these manuscripts was enough to put you to the torture of the Inquisitors. To be actually using the guidance in these works would send you to the stake. There is little doubt that Nostradamus was using his modified version of ancient methods for conjuring up the forces and conditions necessary for him to see the visions. The "it" in the second line of the first quatrain was either a black mirror (a black concave piece of polished metal) or a tray of specially prepared water into which he would gaze. He wrote to his son that the visions came to him in the manner of "imaginative impression" revealed by "God Almighty." Imaginative impression may be exactly what Edgar Cayce was trying to teach to his followers when he encouraged them to develop the "imaginative forces."

In this next quatrain, notice how Nostradamus warns all readers, but notice also that, though he pays homage to the Christian power of his time – and there's much evidence that he genuinely was a believer in Christ – he also allows for other practitioners as long as they are "priest of the rite;" in other words, initiates into the secret teachings and methods.

Let those who read these quatrains reflect maturely
Let the profane, vulgar, and common herd be kept away
Let all – idiot astrologers, non-Christians – stay distant
Who does otherwise, let them be priest of the rite.
(6:100)

Since he was himself an astrologer, the third line must refer to ignorant, mundane astrologers without a clear vision of the cosmos, not all astrologers. We know that Nostradamus prayed, fasted, donned special garments and went through an elaborate preparation ceremony before beginning to gaze into the future – all the trappings of a "priest of the rite."

Nostradamus deliberately obscured the specific

meaning of his prophecies. His quatrains (four-line poems) are not in any sequential order, making it very difficult to establish a clear time-line for the events or to get the whole picture on any particular event or series of events. One literally has to go through the nearly 1,000 quatrains and find everything that appears to refer to a singular major event, such as the Second World War; and then, putting them together, try to establish the sequence of events and people involved. In addition to the mixed arrangement of the quatrains, he deliberately modified names and places using anagrams or ancient and foreign-language names for people and places. And, though he wrote mostly in French, his quatrains are peppered with Latin, Greek, and several other languages. His anagrams for the names of people and places are difficult to see with foresight; much easier to see with hindsight. For example, he sees a new country coming in the distant future (he's viewing from the mid 1500s and seeing into the mid 1700s) and calls this country l'Americh – unmistakably America. He calls a future leader Hister and Ister, which most believe is a reference to Hitler; and the strange name *Pau Nay Loron* is likely the anagram for Napaulon Roy, "Napoleon the King."

In the Preface to his books, called *Centuries*, Nostradamus says that he wrote them "in dark and abstruse sayings ... under a cloudy figure" for fear of controversy. And I would add to these fears the dangers of a population that was so afraid of the unknown that they tended to kill it rather than try to understand it. In fact, Nostradamus was nearly killed by a mob who were spooked by his accurate foresight into the death of their king, Henry II. This was that quatrain:

The young lion will overcome the old one
In single combat on a field of battle

In a golden cage his eyes will be pierced
Two wounds as one, followed by a cruel death (1:35)

The old lion was known in his lifetime to be King Henry II, who used the emblem of the lion (line 1). Shortly after the publication of this quatrain, King Henry II was killed during a joust (line 2) in which his opponent was a young Scottish Captain who also used the emblem of the lion. The young captain's lance splintered upon impact and a piece went through the visor of the golden helmet (cage, line 3) of the old king, piercing his eye and brain, causing him to die a slow and painful death over the next ten days (line 4). An angry mob ran through the streets of Paris looking to burn the prophet for his accuracy – the old "kill the messenger" approach to bad news. Fortunately, Henry's queen was a strong supporter of Nostradamus, so he was spared. The queen turned all attention upon the Captain's role in the death of the king, and it was the Captain that had to escape to England for fear of his life.

Still, it was considered by everyone to be a most accurate prophecy, causing Nostradamus to gain the mixed blessing of fame and suspicion of sorcery. He was right to try to obscure his prophecies so that only those who had the training and wisdom could decipher them.

I am not going to make something out of each quatrain for some are simply too difficult to interpret. Fortunately, there are many quatrains that are very clear in their meaning and to whom and what they refer. It is these quatrains to which we will focus our attention. And it is these quatrains that give us a sense of the timing of changes.

## Prophecies of Earth Changes

Are the prophecies of war and bloodshed, disease and pestilence, famine, drought, flood, and earthquake, prophecies about this century? Here are two quatrains that make one think so:

After great human misery, an even greater approaches
The great motor of the cycles renews
Rain, blood, milk, famine, sword and pestilence
In the sky will be seen a fire with a tail of sparks. (2:46)

Saturn and a water sign in Sagittarius
In its highest increase of exaltation
Pestilence, famine, death from military hand
The century approaches its renewal. (1:16)

The first quatrain seems to be referring to the renewal "cycles" of the millennia, likely the end of one millennium and the beginning of another – for example, the end of 1000s and the beginning of the 2000s. The second appears to be referring to the millennium of the 2000s. Since he was prophesying in the 1500s, we may presume that he wasn't referring backward to 999 but referring forward to 2000. However, I want to share with you that in a letter to his son, Nostradamus clearly says that his prophecies are from "his time to the year 3797 AD." Therefore, his end-times prophecies could be seeing events and changes in the 3000s.

The millennium hysteria caused near panic in 999. Christendom holds closely to the belief that the end of the world will be at the end of a thousand-year period, a millennium, so each millennium is met with high anxiety and expectations. Naturally, those of us who experienced the shift from 1999 to 2000 remember the anxiety felt around the world. Later we will see that the sacred prophecies in Scripture state that the "end times" will be followed by a thousand years when Satan is bound and the world experiences peace and the Messiah will reign. More on this later. Give this sacred prophecy we may wonder if Nostradamus' 3797 could include the final 1,000 years of peace. If 3797 concludes the 1,000 years, then a period from 1797 through 2797 may be the period of Revelation's battle called *Armageddon*, a long struggle between the forces of good and light, and the forces of evil and darkness.

As with all the end times and earth changes prophecies, earthquakes, and floods top the list of predicted events; great fires appear, the loss of major cities, and a pole shift, though this isn't as clear in Nostradamus' writings as it is in Cayce's. Here are some of the quatrains that appear to predict earth changes:

Near Auch, Lectoure, and Mirande
A great fire will fall from the sky for three nights
A thing will happen stupendous and miraculous
And shortly after the ground will tremble. (1:46)

Some interpreters believe this quatrain refers to a comet falling to earth followed by earthquakes. Others believe it refers to our first true visitation by aliens in ships that appear as fires in the night, and their landing causing the ground to shake. The thing that strikes me from this quatrain is the mention of the city of Auch, the capital of ancient Gascony, which included the Pyrenees Mountains. The Cayce visions clearly identify a major cycle beginning in legendary Atlantis, going through ancient Egypt, and continuing to the Pyrenees Mountains, then on to the year 1998. Cayce's teaching is that a new physical body will appear, referencing St. Paul's comment about us all being changed in a "twinkling of an eye" (I Corinthians 15:52). These could be "a thing will happen stupendous and miraculous" (in line 3).

They will think to have seen the sun at night
When the pig, half a man is seen

Noise, chants, battles which appear fought in the sky
And brute beasts will be heard to speak. (1:64)

This is a strange one. It seems to be about an extremely bright light at night, with battles fought in the sky and a pig that is half man, and animals speaking. Animals speaking could be Nostradamus' viewing of our work with dolphins, chimpanzees, and selected birds. The pig that is half man is seen by Erika Cheetham as a modern-day jet pilot in his oxygen mask, helmet, goggles, and flight suit, fighting a battle in the air – which Nostradamus would have seen as very strange. In fact, a battle of this nature may also appear as bright as daylight though it was being fought at night. Jets and bombs make tremendous noise and strange sounds; perhaps rockets and missiles sound like droning chants until they strike (line 3). Cheetham could be right about this one. If so, it is only a view into our times by a 16th century man, having nothing to do with earth changes per se.

The great famine which I see approaching
Turning one way, then another, then becoming universal
So great and long that they will pluck
The roots from the wood and the child from the breast.
(1:67)

Has the world already seen much of this famine? Is it the worldwide Great Depression of the 1930s? Or, is famine moving across the planet, turning one way and then another, ultimately coming to all nations and lands? The last line of this quatrain is reminiscent of Jesus saying "woe to those who nurse babies" during the end times (Matthew 24:19). As I view the African famines on television, those nursing mothers seem sorrowfully helpless, their bodies unable to produce even a minimal nourishment for their babies.

Ennosigee [Earth-shaking] fire from the center of the earth
Will make trembling all around the New City
Two great rocks will long war against each other
Then, Arethusa will color red the new river. (1:87)

Two great rocks warring against each other would be an excellent description of *tectonic plates* creating a seismic fault line. Since Nostradamus precedes this tectonic war with "fire from the center of the earth," I'm inclined to look for volcanic activity to precede the quake and the trembling of the New City. In his time, Paris, London, and Rome were old cities, so it must be one of the newer cities along tectonic plates, perhaps Los Angeles, San Francisco, San Diego, Tokyo, or even New York, though New York's fault has not been warring for a long time. This quatrain seems to fit California cities better than any others.

The name "Arethusa" (line 4) is from Greek mythology. Arethusa was a woodland nymph and one of the attendants of Artemis (goddess of the moon and Apollo's twin sister). Alpheus, a river god, saw her bathing in a stream and tried to embrace her. As she fled under the sea, she called on Artemis for help and was changed into a fountain. It was believed that Alpheus, in the form of a river, flowed underground to Sicily, where he was united with her in the fountain of Arethusa in the city of Syracuse. There is also an orchid/herb called "Dragon's mouth," (its botanical name is *Arethusa bulbosa*). It grows in swamps and bogs from Newfoundland south to North Carolina, and west to Minnesota. Could the "new river" that Arethusa colors red be in these areas? If it is the Midwest of the U.S., then this could be the same prophecy as one of Cayce's, in which he predicts that the Great Lakes will empty into the Gulf of Mexico. That would likely turn the Mississippi red with blood of drowned people working on and living along the river? If this is what Nostradamus saw, then the "new city" he refers to may have been New Madrid.

The Dragon's mouth may well be a reference to increased volcanic activity which precedes the new river's movement. That would be the most dangerous fault along the Mississippi River, the New Madrid Seismic Zone. This leads us directly to the town called New Madrid! This may be Nostradamus' "New City."

Not far from Memphis and St. Louis the continent tried to rip in half 600 million years ago. It failed but left this volatile and super dangerous riff in the middle of the continent. When it moved again, beginning in December of 1811, the town of New Madrid was destroyed, most of it slid under the ground and under water. Huge waves appeared on the Mississippi River overwhelming many boats and washed others high on the shore. High banks collapsed into the river; sand bars and points of islands gave way; whole islands disappeared. In January and February of 1812 more major quakes occurred, from 7.3 to 7.5 magnitude. 2,000 tremors and aftershocks continued into April of 1812. Untold numbers of deaths occurred on the river, turning the water red with blood. The New Madrid earthquakes were the biggest earthquakes on the main land in American history, some registering 7.9 magnitude. They occurred in the central Mississippi Valley, but were felt as far away as New York City, Boston, Montreal, and Washington D.C. President James Madison and his wife Dolly felt them in the White House. Church bells rang in Boston from the rippling vibrations of the ground moving. The Mississippi actually ran backwards for several hours. The earthquakes were preceded by the appearance of a great comet, which was visible around the globe for seventeen months, and was at its brightest during the earthquakes. The comet, with an orbit of 3,065 years, was last seen during the time of Ramses II in Egypt. In 1811-1812, the comet was called "Tecumseh's Comet" by the locals and "Napoleon's Comet" by the Europeans. Thousands of fissures ripped open fields, and geysers burst from the earth, spewing sand, water, mud and coal high into the air. This was surely the "Dragon's mouth" of Arethusa and the color red in the river.

## Terrorism & Nostradamus

Immediately following the terrible attack on the World Trade Center in New York City on September 11, 2001, some people began spreading rumors that Nostradamus had actually written quatrains that prophesied this event. But as cooler heads began to review Nostradamus' writings, no such specific quatrains could be found. But that did not stop some from writing new fake quatrains and attributing them to Nostradamus. Here are two of his actual quatrains which people are quoting. As is often the case with Nostradamus' work, neither of these clearly correlates with the details of the 9/11 terrorist events.

This first quatrain is being misquoted to fit the situation by changing 1999 to "turn of the Century." But the original clearly states the year and month as follows:

In the year 1999 and seven months
From the sky will come a great king of Terror
To resuscitate the great King of the Mongols
Before and after, Mars reigns happily. (10:72)

Let's assume that Nostradamus missed this date by a few years because humanity is making changes in its destiny. He indeed used the word "terror" and identified someone as the "king of terror," which would fit Osama bin Laden and his band of terrorists. Mars, the god of War, would certainly be ruling happily during such times. But how does this quatrain relate to "resuscitating the King of the Mongols"? Could the seer that is viewing from his 16th century perspective be mistaking the Afghans for Mongols? No, because from 16th century France, Afghanistan would be in the land of Mongol Hordes that overran Eastern Europe, Russia, and the Holy Lands in the 12th century. Or could he simply be using poetic license in creating an analogy of the terrible scourge of the Mongols upon Western civilization with the scourge of terrorists in our times? It is possible, but requires some stretching of the words in the original text.

Here is another quatrain circulating:

Forty-five degrees the sky will burn
Fire approaches the grand new city
Instantly a grand flame springs up
When they want to test the Normans. (6:97)

This quatrain may be translated as relating to an event at 45° latitude, but nothing related to this event corresponds to this location. New York City is not on the 45th parallel. We might consider that something is moving at a 45° angle, but nothing corresponds with that either. The jets that struck the Twin Towers were more likely at a 90° angle to the buildings. Bosnia is on the 45th parallel and is a better fit for this quatrain, especially with our accidental bombing of the Chinese Embassy in Bosnia (Chinese being much closer to 12th century Mongols than anyone else). However, the "Normans" is clearly a reference that can be correlated to the New York attack, given that the Normans began the Crusades against the Muslims, and Osama bin

Laden refers in his pronouncements to *Saladin*, the Muslim victor over the Crusaders. His terrorist actions over the past several years have tested the "Normans." The "great new city" may correlate to New York City, but there have been many great new cities from the time of Nostradamus. Bosnia may or may not be one of them.

Wars, disasters, and terrors are throughout Nostradamus' writings and may relate to many events that have happened from his time (1550s).

## The Prophecies of 3 Antichrists

Most interpreters of Nostradamus' quatrains agree that he foresaw three antichrists, namely: Napoleon, Hitler, and someone named "Mabus" and/or "Alus," which are most certainly anagrams or coded versions of the real name or names. Without a doubt, Napoleon and Hitler were destroyers of the world that Nostradamus knew – Europe, England, Russia, Scandinavia and North Africa felt the sting of the bloodshed and devastation of their armies.

Napoleon and Hitler appeared to be a god-send in the beginning of their reign, and the masses would rally behind them with great hope and expectations, only to see them turn into demanding tyrants that would tolerate no opposition; and would send their nation's children into bloody battles with unclear purpose until the death counts were so shocking as to numb the surviving population. Napoleon's wars killed some six million people. Hitler's reign killed more than twelve million – numbers that would surely have shocked Nostradamus.

Here are some of the key quatrains relating to these first two antichrists. Remember, Nostradamus is viewing Napoleon's reign some two hundred years before it occurred, and Hitler's some four hundred years! Yet, his accuracy is amazing. The only way that seeing events hundreds of years before they occur makes any sense is if events occur in some dimension of the mind prior to manifesting in the physical dimension of life. How else could Nostradamus see these physical events before they actually occur and describe them so accurately?

1st Antichrist – Napoleon

Napoleon Bonaparte
(1769-1821; Emperor 1804-1815)

An Emperor will be born near Italy
Who will cost his Empire dearly
They will say, "With what people he keeps company!"
He is less of a prince than a butcher. (1:60)

Napoleon was born on the island of Corsica, very "near Italy" (line 1). He declared himself Emperor, but he was more a war-driven soldier than prince, butchering men was his greatest skill (line 4).

Bearing a name which no French King passed on to him
More fearsome than a thunderbolt
Tremble will Italy, Spain, and England
Of a strange woman greatly attentive. (4:54)

Nostradamus reveals this ruler's non-royal claim to the throne of France and his war-driven power in this quatrain. It is unclear who the strange woman was, perhaps Josephine, though being a traveling soldier, he had many strange women. He also had a strong relationship with his mother. Perhaps she was the strange attentive woman that Nostradamus saw in his dark mirror.

Pau, Nay, Loron more fire than blood will be
In praise to swim, the great man will flee to the confluence.

He will refuse entry to the pies
And the depraved ones of France will keep them
confined. (8:1)

The three names that begin this quatrain are towns in western France. Nostradamus is playing a word game with us. If one rearranges these letters, one gets "Napaulon Roy." Napaulon is the Corsican spelling of Napoleon! Remember, Corsica was his birthplace, so the prophet is giving us another clue. Roy means "King." Interpreters of Nostradamus have pointed out that Napoleon was born under the fire sign, Leo, and, since he was not of the royal bloodline, he was truly "more fire than blood." J.H. Brennan points out that "pies" in line 3 "is a colloquial French diminutive of 'magpies' which, in the original French, shares the same spelling as the name Pius." This links the verse immediately with two Popes, Pius VI and VII, both of whom were actually imprisoned by Napoleon in his capacity as head of what Nostradamus would certainly have considered a "depraved" state (line 4). There is even an explanation of the curious term "confluence" (line 2) in that Pius VI was taken by Napoleon to Valence to die on the confluence of two rivers. This is even clearer in the following quatrain:

Roman Pontiff, beware of approaching
A city which is bathed by two rivers
Your blood will be brought up
You and yours when blooms the rose. (2:97)

Napoleon had Pius VI and thirty-two of his priests taken to Valence, which is bathed by the two rivers Rhone and Isere. There the Pope died, vomiting blood (line 3), and it was on August 29, 1799, the summer season when roses bloom (line 4). How amazing is this vision? It would appear that Nostradamus was actually seeing the scene some 200 years before it physically happened!

In this next quatrain we have a clear description of this Antichrist:

To the Great Empire quite a different man comes
Being distant from kindness and happiness
Ruled by one not long from his bed
While the kingdom to great unhappiness. (6:67)

The "Great Empire" is likely France. And history has described Napoleon as a brooding, lonely, unhappy man (line 2), thus "distant from kindness and happiness." He was strongly influenced by the woman who came to his bed (line 3). That woman was Josephine Rose-Marie Tascher from Martinique. She had a great impact on his decisions and his rise to power and fame. Josephine had high social status which aided Napoleon in his rise to power. Josephine was smart and intelligent. She had a profound influence on Napoleon's emotions in a way that affected his thinking, decisions, and actions. But all the while, the great kingdom of France moved ever closer to disaster, thus "great unhappiness" (line 4).

The end of Napoleon's reign was seen by Nostradamus this way:

The part of Rome ruled by he who interprets the Augur
By the French will be much vexed
But the French nation will rue the hour
of the North Wind [Russia] and the fleet [England] when they drive too far. (2:99)

In ancient Rome the "Augur" was the official seer, using mostly natural signs to interpret future events.

Thus, the Augur saw how Napoleon drove France and her young men too far, gaining the wrath of Rome (lines 1 & 2). The French army would eventually rue the hour that they challenged the deadly winters of Russia (the "North Wind" in line 3) and the British fleet (line 3, victory of British Royal Navy at the Battle of Trafalgar). Ultimately, France was defeated and rued the hour that they began following this Antichrist. But history repeats itself in cycles, for Europe gives life to another great Antichrist that Nostradamus foresaw.

2nd Antichrist – Hitler

Adolf Hitler (1889-1945)
In the following quatrains we read Nostradamus' visions of the coming of another Antichrist who would ravage Europe and beyond, leaving a trail of blood, brutality, and betrayal. He will begin as these antichrists do, by seducing the populous with what they want to hear. Then, he will make them pay dearly for their support.

From the depth of Western Europe
From poor people a child will be born
Who with his tongue will seduce a great crowd of people
His fame increases in the Eastern Kingdom. (3:35)

Hitler was born in Austria, the depths of Western Europe (line 1), to poor parents (line 2). His speeches mesmerized the crowds (line 3). And, his reputation increased his relationship with Japan (the Eastern Kingdom in line 4), resulting in the signing of the Tripartite Pact between Germany, Italy, and Japan.

Again, we have to shocked by how accurate Nostradamus' vision is. He sees specific details about Hitler, his birth, his speaking ability, and his union with an Asian kingdom. And in this next quatrain he very nearly gives us the antichrist's correct name:

Liberty will not be recovered
It will be occupied by a black, fierce, and wicked villain;
When the question of the Pontiff is raised
By D'Hister, the Italian republic will be angry. (5:29)

Once allowed a foothold, Hitler and Nazism never stopped their advance, taking liberty and occupying people's lives and lands with a black, fierce wickedness (lines 1 & 2). Also, the Schutzstaffel, or SS, wore black uniforms and were the elite guard and exterminators for Hitler (line 2). And when the question of the Pope was presented to Hitler, he responded "I will go right into the Vatican!" (line 3) And, of course, under Mussolini and the Tripartite Pact, Hitler and Mussolini angered many freedom-loving Italians. (line 4)

Beasts, driven insane with hunger, will cross the rivers
The greater part of the field will go to Ister
In a cage of iron the great will be dragged away
When the child of Germany observes nothing. (2:24)

"Ister" may be another attempt to get the antichrist's name. Hister and Ister appear to be Nostradamus' struggles with the name. But the details of the evil one's actions are correct. Hitler's armies and their methods and the subsequent governors that ruled in the wake of their victories were like beasts, driven insane with a hunger to possess and purge the world (line 1). In railroad boxcars, many of Europe's great leaders and peoples were dragged away (line 3) by this child of Germany who observed no laws, borders or any form of human decency; nothing (line 4)!

In a spot not too far removed from Venice
The two strongest of Asia and Africa

Will be said to come together with the Rhine and Ister
Weeping at Malta and the Ligurian coast. (4:68)

The Tripartite Axis Pact was signed between Germany, Italy, and Japan at the Brenner Pass, not too far from Venice (line 1). Japan was the "strongest of Asia," Italy annexed Ethiopia, making it the strongest power in Africa (line 2). Malta and Genoa (the Ligurian coast in line 4) were both bombarded heavily during the war; Malta by the Axis powers and Genoa by the Allies.

Just as the French would rue the hour they brought Napoleon to power, so the Germans would pity the day they brought Hitler to power. But it is the bane of humanity that they forget, and so a third Antichrist will rise up, more terrible than the two that preceded him.

### 3rd Antichrist – Mabus and Alus

It is difficult to identify and interpret the quatrains related to this Antichrist, except where Nostradamus clearly uses the names Mabus and Alus, or refers to the Antichrist in a context fitting neither Napoleon nor Hitler. Erika Cheetham suggests that Mabus and Alus may be "corruptions" of the Latin word "Malus," which means "Evil One." Nostradamus only mentions these two names once in separate quatrains. Here are those two quatrains:

Mabus will come, and soon after will die
Of people and beasts a great destruction
Suddenly, vengeance will be seen
Blood, hand, thirst, famine, when a comet passes. (2:62)

His last hand through bloody Alus
Will not save him by sea
Between two rivers he will fear the military hand
The black and wrathful one makes repentant. (6:33)

These quatrains do appear to be very specific. We can see in them that the Antichrist is bloody, destructive, vengeful, and brings famine and thirst. We can also see that a passing comet is a sign of his presence. Somehow, hands play a key role in his activities (line 4 in the first quatrain and lines 1 and 3 in the second). Erika Cheetham has proposed that the "military hand" may be the nuclear "finger on the button" of the 1950s through the 1990s. In line 3 the complete annihilation of humanity. If we jump back to the biblical origin of humanity as seen in the Bible, which Nostradamus would have studied, then humanity began between the two rivers of the Tigris and Euphrates in the Garden of Eden, where Satan in the form of a serpent first gained influence. Perhaps even the Evil One fears the loss of everything, leaving nothing for him to rule, as in line 4: "The black and wrathful one makes repentant." This is a curious statement. Nostradamus uses the French word "noir" here, which most interpreters translate as "black." But noir also means dark. Perhaps this is a reference to the coming day of the Lord, which the Bible says is a time when the sun will not give its light. Noir also has a connotation of darkness as "evil." Perhaps it is a reference to the forces of evil and Satan in the context that St. Paul uses in 1 Corinthians 5:5, "Hand this man over to Satan, so that the sinful nature may be destroyed and his spirit saved on the day of the Lord." In classical theology Satan was employed by God to test us, as in Job 1:12, where God instructs Satan to test Job to see if his heart and motivations are spiritual or simply materialistic.

If we are measuring by the number of violent deaths, then the 1900s have been the deadliest century in human history – and there have been many, many deadly centuries. It has been estimated that some 200 million people lost their lives through human acts of oppression which led to violence, famine, and disease in the 20th Century. Some of this evil the world has never seen before. Few nations on the earth have avoided a role in this bloodshed during this period. And as for the passing comet, it would certainly appear to be Nostradamus' way of *dating* the coming of this Antichrist. Unfortunately, there are many comets, and many have come and gone when the world seemed in great peril. Nostradamus did specifically write about the Antichrist and persons acting like an Antichrist. Here's a quatrain to consider, and it has a very specific date:

In the year 1999 and seven months
From the sky will come a great King of Terror
To resuscitate the great King of the Mongols
Before and after, Mars reigns happily (10:72)

Certainly, this is one of the clearest dates in the whole of Nostradamus' work. And it is again striking how he could see so far in the future and give a specific date for the event.

It appears to fit the prophecies of the Armageddon, in Edgar Cayce's visions, described as a battle fought in the "air" (line 2, "from the sky") between the forces of good and evil.

The resuscitating of the King of the Mongols (line 3) is a terrible thought. History still holds the Mongol Hordes and their reign throughout all of Asia and much of Europe during the 1200s as one of the most brutal, cruel, barbarous periods ever. It has been estimated that Genghis Khan (1206-1227) killed 40 million in his reign of terror! India, Persia, Arabia, Russia, and Eastern Europe all suffered the murderous brutality of these conquerors. These barbarians nearly wiped out Islam, and when the Mongols defeated the armies of Western

Europe, the Vatican and the Holy Land were defenseless to their invasion, all of Christendom appeared to be lost. Then, a miracle happened. The great Khan died! To everyone's shock, the Mongol hordes returned home to mourn and fight among themselves, leaving much of the conquered lands to recover and rebuild.

If we are to assume from this quatrain that these cruel souls are to rise again from the dead to spread their uncaring brutality across the planet, then this is the worst of Nostradamus' predictions, suited well to Jesus' statement that lawlessness will reign so freely that the hearts of many will grow cold (Matthew 24:12). However, no world event in July 1999 would meet this level of terror. It is possible that seeing some 400 years into the future could not account for small shifts in the timeline of events. He may have actually been viewing September 2001, when out of Afghanistan terrorists attacked the World Trade Center – a large complex of seven buildings in Lower Manhattan, New York City, United States. It featured the landmark Twin Towers, which were destroyed in the attack. Nostradamus would have seen Afghanistan as part of the Mongol Empire. And this event truly did give birth to terrorism around the world in these times, making the god of war, Mars, happy.

Nostradamus also saw the rise of a leader who declares Thursday as his holy day. Islam has Friday, Judaism Saturday, and Christianity Sunday; but this new leader will apparently reform some current religion or develop a new one with Thursday as the holy day. It is not clear if this person is an Antichrist or a good leader, but there are some hints:

From the aquatic triplicity will be born
One who will have Thursday for his holy day

His fame, praise, rule and power will grow
By land and sea to become a tempest to the Orient.
(1:50)

"From the aquatic triplicity" could mean the three water signs of the zodiac: Cancer, Scorpio and Pisces. Perhaps these will be predominant in his horoscope. Or, as Henry Roberts suggests, perhaps the aquatic triplicity is the Atlantic, Pacific and Gulf of Mexico; in other words, the U.S.A. with Thanksgiving as its special day, the last Thursday of November. Certainly the U.S. has been giving the Orient (line 4) much attention: China in the early 1900s, Japan in the 40s, Korea in the 50s, Vietnam in the 60s and 70s, Taiwan and again China in the 80s, and again China and North Korea in recent years. The U.S. has had many ongoing interactions with the Orient, good and bad, by land and sea (line 4). In this case then, the man in the quatrain could be Franklin D. Roosevelt who officially declared Thanksgiving (4th Thursday of November) as a U.S. national holiday. This is supported by another quatrain that does appear to foreshadow the founding of the new, "fair" land to which many will come and give honor, namely America. This new country begins in the freezing cold winters of Plymouth, Massachusetts which leads to the special Thursday of Thanksgiving.

The land and air will freeze with so much water
When they come to venerate Thursday
That which will be, never was so fair
Of the four quarters they will come to honor him. (10:71)

If this is what these quatrains are referring to, then Nostradamus' visions, seen in the mid 1500s, are truly amazing. Nevertheless, I'd keep my eye open for someone else declaring Thursday as his holy day. Surprisingly, we have another holy day to watch for:

The penultimate one of the surname of the Prophet
Will take Monday for his day of rest
Wandering far because of his frenzied head
Delivering a great people from impositions. (2:28)

*Penultimate* means "next to last," and a surname is a name held by all members of a family. "The Prophet" is usually a reference to Mohammed, but I don't see how this leads to any conclusions. It's difficult to know exactly what Nostradamus meant. The least we can say is that Nostradamus saw two leaders using Monday and Thursday, as their rest day and holy day. All we can do is wait and see how this plays out on the world stage.

There are only two quatrains where the term "Antichrist" is used plainly.

By the Antichrist, three will be quickly annihilated
Twenty-seven years of blood will last his war
The heretics dead, captive, exiled
Bloody human corpses, water red, covering the earth. (8:77)

The chief of London by l'Americh [American] power
The isle of Scotland burdened with ice [frost?]
Roy Reb will have so dreadful an Antichrist
Who will put them all in discord. (10:66)

Could the "three" (line 1) of the first quatrain be the same as the three in the second quatrain, namely, London, America, and Scotland? Or is Scotland only used as a sign that a major climate change has occurred, putting Scotland under ice and an island separated from the English mainland (line 2)?

Who or what is Roy Reb? Roy means "king," but Reb is unclear. In Judaism, Reb is a form of Rabbi. Perhaps Nostradamus is speaking of a great deceiver that leads the Jews astray or in discord with one another. However, I don't see how this relates to the first two lines of this quatrain. Of course, the 27-year-long war in the first quatrain could easily relate to the Jews, because they've been in a virtual war since the sixties; and if Nostradamus considers the Islamic opponents to be "heretics" to the teachings of Father Abraham, then his lines about "The heretics dead, captive, exiled (one of Israel's common punishments). "Bloody human corpses, water red (Red Sea?), covering the earth" has relevance to this Middle Eastern battle that has been raging for so long, and involving the whole earth in its problems.

Some interpreters say it's Rob Roy of Scotland (1671-1734), a Robin Hood character who rustled cattle and sold his neighbors protection. I don't see how that relates to these quatrains. Erika Cheetham believes the second quatrain relates to U.S. nuclear weapons being housed on Scottish soil with the permission of the chief of London, which caused much discomfort for these three governments, mostly from their own people. Actually, I'm inclined to take a broader interpretation of these two quatrains.

The Antichrist is, as Edgar Cayce stated, a spirit, an attitude with chillingly violent, uncaring, unthinking emotions that insidiously creeps into the hearts and minds of individuals, families, communities, nations and leaders, blocking out the light of Christ (which is the love of God and one's neighbor) and bringing on the conditions necessary for "bloody human corpses, red water and discord" everywhere. Could the "three quickly annihilated" by the Antichrist be "faith, hope and charity?" Could Roy Reb be just that, King Reb or Rebel – that spirit that separates oneself from a sense of oneness with others and God, allowing us to do whatever seems good to us, with complete disregard for what others might want or need, or what the Christ spirit wants? Jesus says the end times will cause hearts to grow cold; even the elect would fall away if the end time were not shortened (Matthew 24). If we consider that Nostradamus used anagrams and word-plays, the terms Mabus and Alus could be:

"May-b-us" and "All us"

Is it possible that the Antichrist, no matter who personifies this spirit as a leader, requires us to give it fuel, to give it life in our hearts and minds? Notice in this quatrain how American power makes it happen. America is where the governing influence is by the people and for the people. If the people become tainted by mean-spiritedness, spitefulness, revenge, intolerance, etc., then the Antichrist has gained power. The power is with the people, each of us, in our hearts and minds. We then give power to families, communities, nations and leaders. What spirit will rule? As God said in Genesis, Evil's "desire is for you, but you must master it." Or, "Go. Be fruitful and multiply, but subdue the earth" and its influence upon us.

May be us, all of us, is a dark spirit that takes hold of our free wills and high responsibility, leading us and the world into a dark place.

### Nostradamus' Long-term Vision

Critics of Nostradamus' work say that almost anything can be predicted using his quatrains because they are so open to interpretation. I've tried to select those that have some specificity to them.

Here's one of his quatrains that indicates that life on this planet will go on for some time into the distant future:

Twenty years of the moon's reign pass

Seven thousand years another monarch shall hold
When the sun takes up his days
Then shall my prophecies be complete. (1:48)

Seven thousand years is a long time. I believe we have many more adventures to enjoy and make the most of before the final end comes. What we are approaching now is a great change from one era to another. It may be challenging and transforming, but as Jesus said, it is only the "birth pains" of the delivery of a new age of hope and peace (Matthew 24:8).

Michel de Nostradame, Nostradamus

The Newspaper report for the day of
the Fatima Miracle in Portugal

## Prophecies of Mary, the Mother of Jesus

There are hundreds of reported appearances of the Virgin Mary, the Mother of Jesus. "Apparition" has become the word used to describe these visions, a word that means, "to unexpectedly appear, to become visible without warning or preparation." It also refers to "a phantom or ghost." Everyone that has reported seeing the image agrees that it is not physical, is surrounded by light, sound, and movement that is not normal, and appears without warning or invitation. The seers are usually engaged in everyday activities when suddenly she appears. Lightning or a clap of thunder sometimes accompanies her appearance. In some cases, the appearance of a male "light-being," or angel precedes her. Sometimes the angel has identified himself as the archangel Michael, whom we know as the archangel of the heavenly battle against Lucifer. The Female-image identifies herself in different ways, calling herself at different times: The Lady of Peace, The Queen of Peace, The Immaculate Heart; to the children in Rwanda, Africa she called herself "The Mother of the World," which appears to be a clear reference to Genesis' name for Eve, "The Mother of All."

There are some consistent features to these apparitions. She is always bright with light, a veil over her head, wearing a seamless dress (often white, once blue, once in Aztec garments), barefoot, and able to move without walking, most describe her movement as "gliding." She is always suspended above the ground, and appears and disappears with great speed. As mentioned earlier, lightning and/or thunder, or some unusual sound with light usually accompanies her appearance. Colors frequently associated with her appearances are starlight white and sky blue.

Her appearance and language have a universal quality to them. The black children to whom she appeared in Africa could not recall what "color" her skin was. They described her as being "like them," but not black, white, or "half-caste." To the white girls in Medjugorje, Yugoslavia, her skin color was not discernable, except that she was not white like her pictures, but neither was she any other color. She spoke in the native language of each group that saw her – Tolpetlac, Spanish, French, Portuguese, Slavic, Rwandan, English, and so on.

Overall, her teachings are universal in their tone and content, supporting no specific faith or doctrine. For example, to the children in Medjugorje she said, "There is only one God and one Faith." To the children in Rwanda she said, "Before God there is neither Protestant nor Catholic, nor Adventist, nor Moslem, nor any branch of other creeds. The true son of God is whoever does God's will." A Catholic priest in the Rwandan school where the apparitions occurred notes that "the Lady" never asked the Protestant or Moslem pupils to "become Catholic, but to recognize her as the Mother of God."

A peculiar and fascinating fact about these apparitions is the progression of the time of day that she appeared beginning before dawn in the Guadalupe apparition in 1531, morning in Lourdes in 1858, noon in Fatima in 1917, evening in Medjugorje in 1981 and the nightfall appearances later that same year in Rwanda. This progression fits with ancient mystical teachings that the progression of the Sun through the heavens reflects the progression of humanity through the Earth.

The earliest of her apparitions that I could find was to the apostle James in Saragossa, Spain in 40 A.D., instructing him to build a church there. In 1251 A.D. she appeared to Simon Stock (later St. Simon) at Aylesford, Kent. In this apparition she identified herself as "Our Lady of Mt. Carmel," a name the archangel Michael also used for her during the apparitions at Garabandal in 1961. Mt. Carmel was the ancient site of the Essene Temple (a sect of the Jewish faith at the time of Christ), where, according to the Cayce visions, women served as equals with men. The Essenes had a rare sense of the Divine Feminine and its representation in woman. The Cayce visions also said that Mary, the mother of Jesus, was trained and chosen at the Temple in Mt. Carmel.

She appears again in 1475 at Bétharram and in 1510 at Garaison, both in the Pyrenees Mountains. This is the first of a long and important series of apparitions in the Pyrenees. Note how significant this is when we consider Cayce's teaching that the great path we have been walking has led from the ancient lands of Atlantis and Egypt to "the Death of the Son of Man as a man," then to the Pyrenees, and finally to 1998 (see Cayce section in this book for details).

Let's focus our attention on three of the hundreds of apparitions, dating from 1917 to 1986 because they have much prophecy. These occurred at Fatima, Garabandal, and Medjugorje.

Some of you may wonder why I would skip over one of the most famous apparitions occurring in 1858 in Lourdes, France (continuing the line of Pyrenees apparitions). From February 18th to March 4th, Bernadette saw a glowing girl 18 times in a grotto with a healing spring. Many, many healings have occurred at this sacred grotto but as far as the prophetic aspect of the apparitions at Lourdes, Bernadette says the glowing girl who identified herself as "The Immaculate Conception," told her "secrets" of things to come and what she (the glowing girl) was going to do. However, little of the content of these secrets is known. Therefore, we focus on apparitions with lots of prophecy, especially prophecy for our times.

## Fatima, Portugal 1917

"A strong wind began to shake the trees," recalls Lucia, who was nine years old when this happened. "Then, we began to see in the distance, above the trees that stretched to the east, a light whiter than snow, in the form of a young man, quite transparent, and as brilliant as crystal." She and her companions, eight-year-old Francisco and six-year-old Jacinta, watched in wonder as the light being approached them. It said to them, "Do not be afraid. I am the Angel of Peace. Pray with me." They knelt beside him on the bare spot of dirt next to a large white stone, and repeated after him, "My God, I believe, I adore, I hope, and I love You. I ask forgiveness for those who do not believe, nor adore, nor hope, nor love You." Then he was gone.

They returned to their village but told no one of their experience. His coming had left them with a strange feeling of heaviness and portent. In their hearts they wondered, and continued that strange prayer.

Later in the summer, he came again, this time to Lucia's back yard. He asked, "What are you doing? You must pray! Pray!," explaining to the children that their prayers could bring peace to Portugal. Lucia, Francisco and Jacinta prayed everyday with great intensity and devotion. That autumn he came again. This time he came with the Holy Grail, the Chalice of Communion, which he left suspended in midair as he knelt with them again to pray. Rising from prayer, the light being gave the Communion Host to Lucia, as the body of Christ, and the Chalice to Jacinta and Francisco, as the blood of Christ. As he did this he said, "Take and drink the Body and Blood of Jesus Christ, horribly outraged by ungrateful men. Repair their crimes and console your God."

When the angel had gone, there was only silence. None of them spoke. Sealed in this special moment, they simply sat together in the quiet.

But life goes on, and eventually the children returned to their normal routines of school, play, and chores. The following Spring, May 13, 1917 to be exact, they were tending sheep in the pasture, nearly a mile-and-a-half from home, when it happened again, but with an amazing twist.

At noon, from out of a clear, blue sky came what appeared to be two flashes of lightning. It startled the children. They turned in unison, and above a small holm-oak tree was the figure of a young lady, about sixteen years old, all alight, glowing with a sparkling radiance of light. It appeared that a star was actually wrapped in the folds of her dress. At first the light seemed too brilliant to look into for long, but the children adjusted to the radiance, and gradually more details of the lady were visible. She was wearing a white mantle with gold edges over her head. Her dress was blue, like the sky. When Lucia asked who she was, she simply answered "I have come from heaven." She told the children that she would tell them exactly who she was on October 13th; until then, they were to come to this spot on the 13th of each month and pray. Then she asked, "Will you offer yourselves to God and bear all the sufferings He sends you, in atonement for the sins that offend Him, and for the conversion of sinners?" The children enthusiastically responded, "Oh, we will! We will!" "Then," she said, "you will have a great deal to suffer, but the grace of God will be with you and will strengthen you. Say the rosary every day to bring peace to the world and an end to war." In a blaze of light, the lady disappeared to the east.

Little Jacinta could not keep silent any longer. The light man, or angel, always filled her with a heavy sense of omen, or something dreadful coming. But the light lady filled her with happiness and life. After supper that night, Jacinta told her mother. Little did Jacinta know how the adult world was going to react. Her parents spoke with Francisco's parents, and they all spoke with the parents of the eldest child, Lucia. Lucia's mother was furious and horrified. She believed her daughter had created a terrible hoax, and the whole village would know about it! She beat, begged, and ordered her daughter to recant this disgraceful lie. These were hard times for the children. Reality had raised its powerful head, and there was no room for beings from heaven.

Finally, a month had passed and it was time to return to the site on the 13th of June. The children's parents would not go with them, but some of the villagers came along. To everyone's surprise, the lightning flashed in the midst of the noonday sun and the light lady appeared above the little holm-oak tree. She spoke to the children, saying, "I want you to continue saying the rosary every day. And after each one of the mysteries, my children, I want you to pray in this way: 'O my Jesus, forgive us and deliver us from the fire of hell. Take all souls to heaven, especially those in greatest need.'" Lucia, perhaps weary of the Earth's harsh reaction to her claims of heavenly visions, asked the Lady, "Will you take us to heaven?" Surprisingly, the Lady answered, "Yes. I will take Jacinta and Francisco soon, but you will remain a little longer, since Jesus wishes you to make me known and loved on Earth. He wishes also for you to establish devotion in the world to my Immaculate Heart."

The crowd who knelt around the children saw the lightning, but not the apparition. However, they could hear a small voice speaking in response to Lucia's comments and questions, but could not make out what it was saying. Above the tree, they saw only a little cloud. When Lucia said the Lady was leaving, the crowd saw the little cloud rise very slowly and move off to the east. This, however, was enough phenomena to make the children celebrities. Unfortunately, to some people, they were notorious celebrities of the ridiculous! Strangers and neighbors began to ridicule and taunt the children. People in authority questioned them over and over for every weary detail, looking for the flaw in their stories. Lucia's mother and the local priest had almost convinced Lucia that she had been duped by the Devil! The little girl was in torment over the whole thing. It was as the light Lady had foretold, the children suffered much for what they had seen. Lucia had actually decided not to go on the 13th of the next month.

On July 13th, the village of Fatima was shocked when hundreds of seekers from all over came to their village to join with the children in the vigil for the Lady of Light. It was a hot summer day. The sun was blinding. However, at noon, the sun paled, though the sky was cloudless and blue. Silence swept through the crowds as they began to hear "a little buzzing sound." Many saw a little ball of light settle above the tiny holm-oak tree. But the sight of the Lady and the sound of her voice were only seen and heard by the children. Not surprisingly, Lucia came at the last minute, driven by something inside of her, despite all the terrible repercussions that were sure to follow.

The Lady repeated her request for prayer to end war and bring peace to the world, and promised that she would reveal her identify on October 13th. She gave another prayer, "O Jesus, this is for the love of thee, for the conversion of sinners, and in reparation for sins committed against the Immaculate Heart of Mary." Then, she told the children a threefold secret. This was followed by a view into the nature of Hell, which the Lady sadly said, "Where the souls of sinners go. It is to save them that God wants to establish in the world devotion to my Immaculate Heart. If you do what I tell you, many souls will be saved, and there will be peace." Then followed a prophecy of the fate of humanity and of nations from 1917 into the future. With a clap of thunder the vision was over.

The crowd pressed in upon the children, some seeking to touch their garments, some to spit into their little faces and mock them. The cruelty of the unbelievers was shocking. Lucia's mother beat her with a broom stick. Every woman in the village deemed it their duty to slap sense into these crazy, trouble-making children. These little ones could go nowhere without physical and emotional abuse and torment.

On the 13th of September, the children were much weary of the world's oppressive reaction to their visions of heaven and light beings. They had suffered at the hands of cruel, condemning people, even among their own loved ones. When the Lady appeared that month, Lucia began with this pleading request, "So many believe that I am an impostor and a cheat that they say I deserve to be hanged and burned. Will you please perform a miracle so that all of them can believe?" Just as Jesus was always asked to show the doubters a sign, so little Lucia was now asking the Lady to show her a sign. When the Lady agreed to show all a sign on October 13th, the children proclaimed it openly, believing that everyone would begin to act differently. To their surprise, the ridicule and abuse increased. As the date approached, the newspapers were printing satirical stories about "the three little deceivers." Freemason groups and civic groups threatened to bomb the children's homes. In the night, Lucia's distraught mother would wake her from sleep, shaking her and demanding that she confess her fantasy before it was too late.

Finally, October 13th arrived. Seventy thousand people crammed into the pasture to witness the event! Some came to see the farce, others to witness a miracle from God. It was bitter cold. Rain fell all night and into the day. Thousands of black umbrellas created an eerie scene across the pasture. Many prayed and chanted. The rain grew intense. Gray, wet and cold was the aura of that day. Exactly at noon, the children fell to their knees, with chins turned upward, rain pouring onto their faces. They were obviously looking at and listening to something. Throughout the vision Mary prophesied things to come and instructions that must be followed. In the vision she identified herself as had been promised back on May 13th, saying, "I am the Lady of the Rosary," which of course we know is Mary (most of the beads on a rosary are for the prayer, "Hail Mary").

Then the miracle occurred above the large crowd who had gathered. People witnessed extraordinary solar activity, such as the sun appearing to "dance" or zig-zag in the sky, careen towards the earth, and emit multi-colored light in radiant colors. According to these reports, the event lasted approximately ten minutes. After years of gathering eye-witness interviews and reports Bishop José da Silva declared the miracle "worthy of belief" on 13 October 1930, and it became an officially recognized appearance of Mary and her miracle by the Church.

Our focus here is on the prophecies that Mother Mary delivered at Fatima and many other places and times throughout this century. To the Fatima children she confided the following:

### The Prophecies of Fatima
1. Evil, sin, and hell-like torment do indeed exist, despite the fashionable ideas to the contrary. Evil-doers, sinners, abiders in hell, and lost souls must soon begin to turn from their ways and catch hold of God's light

and love, before it is too late. The children felt an ominous implication in all of this. Something is going to happen, and it's going to happen soon. Everyone had better get their house in order and their hearts right with God. Also, all seekers of God should pray for the conversion of evil and lost souls.

2. World War I will end within one year if you pray for peace. WWI ended with the signing of an armistice on November 11, 1918. However, the "war that was to end all wars" (WWI) would be followed by an even worse war. The evil of this war would be preceded by a great light in the sky, which many in Europe saw. She also said the war would occur during the reign of a Pope named "Pius XI" (specifically named by the Lady). At the time of this prophecy, the reigning Pope was Benedict XV. WWII began in 1936, during the reign of Pius XI.

In this year, 1917, the Lady prophesied that a great battle for the heart of Russia was engaged. At this time in history, Russia was still a strong religious country, mostly Eastern Orthodox Catholic. The Lady said, "If Russia consecrates herself to the Immaculate Heart, then there will be peace. If not, then Russia will spread her errors throughout the world, bringing new wars and persecution ... Certain nations will be annihilated." All of us who have the benefit of hindsight know that Russia became the Soviet Union, gobbling up nations and peoples everywhere. Bolshevik-style Communism became the dark banner under which she traveled the world, creating her "Soviet Bloc." In 1917, Communism was simply a theory, not a threat, but the Bolshevik revolution was about to take a big step. Little did the world know how powerful and menacing Bolshevik Communism would become in future decades, right up until the fall of the Soviet Union in the 1980s. In recent times, religion is making a comeback in a broken and struggling Russia, and nations that had been gobbled up in the Union of Soviet Socialist Republic, are once again independent.

Mary gave her last appearance and warning on October 13, 1917; and the Bolshevik revolution began for real on October 25, 1917 (old style dating, November 7th new style dating)! The Christian Church in Russia was cruelly dismantled, much of it destroyed forever, many priests and holy people murdered, and the faith lost to Communist atheism.

However, I interviewed many Roman Catholics who shared that all through their schooling and worship they were instructed to pray for Russia, believing that Mary's promises that prayer could save Russia would be fulfilled. Their prayers appear to have succeeded. Beginning in the late 1980s, under Mikhail Gorbachev, the new political and social freedoms resulted in many church buildings being returned to the church, to be restored by local parishioners. A pivotal point in the history of the Russian Orthodox Church came in 1988. Throughout the summer of that year major government-supported celebrations took place in Moscow and other cities; many older churches and some monasteries were reopened. An implicit ban on religious propaganda on state TV was lifted. For the first time in the history of the Soviet Union, people could see live transmissions of church services on television.

### Garabandal, Spain 1961

On June 18, 1961, 13-year-old Maria Concepcion Gonzalez's (nicknamed, Conchita) recorded the following story:

"Suddenly, there appeared to me a very beautiful figure that shone brilliantly but did not hurt my eyes at all. When the other three girls Jacinta, Loli and Mari Cruz saw me in this state of ecstasy, they thought that I was having a fit, because I kept saying, with my hands clasped: 'Ay! Ay! Oh! Oh!' They were about to call my mother when they found themselves in the same state as I, and cried out together: 'Ay! Oh! The angel!'

"There was a short silence among the four of us. Then, all of a sudden, the angel disappeared and we returned to normal. Greatly frightened, we ran toward the church. As we passed the dance that was going on in the village, a girl named Pili Gonzalez said to us, 'You look pale and scared!' We said together, 'It is because we have seen an angel!' 'Is it true?' she asked. We said together, 'Yes, yes!'

"Then we continued on in the direction of the church. When we arrived at the church, we went around back and cried. Some little girls playing there asked, 'Why are you crying?' We said, 'Because we saw an angel.'" They ran off to tell the schoolmistress.

"When we stopped crying, we went into the church. The schoolmistress arrived in a very frightened state and asked us, "Is it true that you have seen an angel?' We simply replied, 'Yes, yes.' She then led us on a station [this is the Stations of the Cross, a series of prayers before pictures of the various stages Jesus went through in his arrest, scourging, crucifixion, death and resurrection], giving thanks to Jesus in the Blessed Sacrament.

"When we finished the station, we all went home. My mother wanted me home before dark, but it was now nine o'clock and dark. She said, 'Haven't I told you that you should get home while it is still daylight?'

"I was very upset by these two things having seen such a beautiful figure and having arrived home late. I don't dare go into the kitchen. I lean up against the door post and say, 'I've seen an angel.'

"Mother says, 'Coming home late, you come in here and tell me things like that!'

"'But I did see an angel!'

"We didn't say anything more about the matter that evening. The rest of the time was spent in the usual manner without talking about anything at all."

But the next day would prove to be a different situation. The word had spread all over town about four hysterical girls who had run to the church crying because they had seen something. Now the questioning and ridicule was to begin. Much of it occurred on the way to school by older children and adults. Once in school, however, their peers were very interested in all the details. School let out at one o'clock, and on their way home the town pastor caught up with them. He believed that they might have made a mistake in their assumption that it was an angel.

Separating Conchita from the other children, the pastor demanded that Conchita be honest about this whole thing. But there was a nervousness about the priest that caused Conchita to recite every moment and detail of the event to him carefully. She noticed how attentively he listened. When she was done, he demanded that she ask the angel-like being to identify himself – that is, if he came again.

The pastor questioned each of the other children separately as he had Conchita. It was obvious to all that he was becoming more certain the children had seen something special. But he told everyone that he would wait to see if any more appearances occurred before he told the Bishop.

The next days went by as most other days. Except for the visitors and the questions, life was normal school, play, and meals until the girls desired to return to the spot. This upset their families. The overall feeling was to stay away from trouble; don't go looking for it. Conchita's mother started crying about "the mess." Life had been going just fine until this angel stuff. Conchita writes in her diary that she asked her mother to suppose it was true. "What then?" she asked. This reflection caused her mother to let her go to the spot again.

Conchita called the spot "a corner of heaven" (un trocito de cielo). But on their way, the people made fun of them, asking "Why don't you go to the church to pray rather than that alley?" Some of the people actually tried to chase the children away, but they would not go. Then, as the children prayed, others began throwing stones at them. The children endured this, continuing to pray. After a long time, it became evident that the angel wasn't coming. As the children walked home, the schoolmistress met them and asked if they had been to the alley. When they explained that they had and that nothing had happened, she responded as though it was common knowledge that the angel didn't come because it was very cloudy!

As the days passed without another appearance, more and more people began to think that it had all been the children's imagination; even the children themselves were beginning to wonder.

The original appearance had occurred at about 8:30 p.m., but since it was summer, it was still light. Two days later the children happened to get together again. So, they decided to try again. In the alley they prayed their rosary and then, as they were leaving for their homes, a bright light began to shine. It was so bright that the children could no longer see each other. Unfortunately, they became frightened and began to scream. The brilliant light disappeared.

The next day, the children tried again. This time when the angel appeared, the children remained calm. They even asked him who he was and why he had come. He did not answer. The appearance was over shortly. But everyone watching the girls was now convinced that they were seeing something very special.

The evening of the 22nd, near the usual time, 8:30

p.m., the angel appeared again. The surrounding people only saw the children go into ecstasy. They saw no other phenomena. However, the expression on the children's faces caused an excitement to spread through the crowd, and the people began to shout, *Era cierto!*, "It was true!"

As usual, the crowds attracted the police, and the police began to look for causes beyond heavenly ones. Hypnosis was suspected and a charge was made against these girls and a man of the town who had been at the scene, and who knew and practiced hypnosis. They wanted to put him in jail. But many in the crowd were convinced that it was not hypnosis, and testified that the man had nothing to do with the children before or during the appearance, so the police took no action.

During the next appearance, which was a little earlier in the evening, many of the authorities were present. Their disbelief caused them to do many cruel things to these children. Conchita's own doctor lifted her up during the ecstasy (she was in a kneeling position) and dropped her from a height of 3 feet onto the stone street to see if she was faking it. There was a noise like cracking bones that caused many onlookers to cringe. Her legs remained bent in the kneeling position throughout the incident. She was obviously not aware of what had just happened to her knees and remained in her ecstatic state. When she returned to normal consciousness, some concerned ladies began to examine and care for her knees.

Afterward, the authorities took the children to the church, isolated them, and began to interrogate them.

On the 26th and 27th, word had spread far and wide, and many people came to witness the angelic appearance. However, nothing happened. Disillusionment filled the crowd and the children. The believers were disappointed and the non-believers were filled with the pride of their certainty about things like this.

Conchita remembers thinking, "If God wants it that way, that is the way it must be."

On the 28th, the angel appeared again, but this time at nine o'clock, and the ecstasy lasted until 10 o'clock. The angel was very happy at the faith and persistence of the children and their supporters, but did not say this or anything else. The children could simply sense his feelings. He appeared again and again over the next few days, until July 1, when he finally spoke.

"Do you know why I have come?" the angel asked. "It is to announce to you that tomorrow, Sunday, the Virgin Mary will appear to you as Our Lady of Mount Carmel." The children replied, "We hope she comes soon!" The angel only smiled. Then the angel spoke with the children *for two hours*, but it felt like only a few minutes to the children.

Much of the conversation was friendly and casual, with the angel asking them if they remembered how concerned they had become when first they saw Conchita "have a fit," and were going to go get her mother? The children told the angel it was because she looked so strange. Then they all, including the angel, laughed. Finally, the angel said he would return tomorrow with the "Blessed Virgin."

Unlike the children's experiences at Fatima, the appearances of the angel at Garabandal caused the children great joy and fulfillment. You'll recall the Fatima children, especially the youngest, felt great foreboding when in the presence of the angel. The Garabandal children only felt sadness after he left, wishing they could stay in his presence always.

During this appearance, the children noticed "a sign" that they had also seen in one of the previous appearances. Below the angel was a banner. On it were some words and below them were some Roman numerals: "It is necessary that XVII MCMLXI." (17 1961)

In the previous appearance, the children simply did not want to take their eyes off the angel long enough to clearly see the banner. But in this appearance, they had plenty of time. They even asked the angel what it meant, to which he replied that the Virgin would tell them.

During this appearance the children also discerned more details of the angel's features and clothing. In her diary, Conchita describes him as follows:

"The angel was dressed in a long, flowing, blue garment without a belt. His wings were pale rose, long and very lovely. His little face was not long or round. His nose was very pretty. His eyes black and his skin dark. His hands were very delicate and his fingernails short. We did not see his feet."

On Sunday, July 2, 1961, the town was packed with people from all over. From the church, the girls and the crowd headed for the alley, but never made it. Along the way, around 6 p.m., the Blessed Virgin appeared with an angel on each side of her. One of them was Michael the archangel, whom the children knew. The other angel they did not recognize, but he was dressed exactly like Michael. The children thought they looked like twins. Next to the unknown angel was a large eye, which the children thought was the eye of God.

Conchita's dairy describes the Lady this way:

"The Blessed Virgin appeared in a white dress, a blue mantle with a crown of small golden stars above her head. Her feet were not visible. Her hands were wide open. Her hair is long, dark brown and wavy, and parted in the middle. She has an oval shaped face and her nose is long and delicate. Her mouth is very pretty with rather full lips. The color of her face is dark, but lighter than the angel's, it's different. Her voice is very lovely, a very unusual voice that I can't describe. There is no woman that resembles the Blessed Virgin in her

69

voice, or anything else. In her arms she sometimes carries the baby Jesus. He is very tiny, like a newborn with a little face. His complexion is like that of the Blessed Virgin's."

From this apparition on, everyone close to the girls, including most of the townspeople and the pastor, believed and supported them. Their parents actually began to prepare and remind the children that the hour (6 p.m.) was approaching and they should get to the spot and begin praying. However, the children began to realize that in the past they always were "called" to come to the site. This was a surprise to everyone. The children explained that they "heard" an inner voice, but not with their ears, nor were their names actually called. In fact, there were three types of calling! One was a feeling of joy stirring within them. Another was stronger, with a noticeable sense of excitement rising within them. And the final and most powerful calling was a full, almost overwhelming feeling of excitement and happiness. The children said that they usually departed for the site on the second calling.

Not surprisingly, when the girls had finished describing the calls, they got a call! As is so common, the adult doubters still tried to test the girls. They came up with a plan to separate the girls in different homes, and then see if all four got the "calling" at the same time. A half-hour after being separated, all four girls got the second calling at the same time and arrived at the new site of the apparitions at the same time. This really did amaze many of the doubters.

As soon as they arrived, the apparition occurred. It was 7 p.m. The Virgin Mary had the baby Jesus in her arms, but the angels were nowhere to be seen. Some of the people who had come with the children had given them objects for the Blessed Mother to kiss, and she kissed all of them. They asked to hold the baby Jesus, but both the baby and Mother only smiled at the request. She disappeared saying, "Tomorrow, you will see me again."

The kissed objects had the sweet scent of perfume about them. Everyone was excited. During the apparition, the observers saw the girls playing with what appeared to be a baby, but they didn't actually see the baby.

It is interesting to note that the Garabandal girls never mentioned in their statements or journals any bright light or luminosity around the Blessed Mother. She appeared in clear form. However, the children do say that though she kissed them good-bye, they never really felt a physical contact to their heads, and when holding the baby they felt pressure but not physical contact. It was not a physical presence, or body, yet everything else about it seemed real.

On October 18th, we receive the first message from the Blessed Mother. Actually, the message was given to the children on July 4th, but they were to reveal it publicly after the apparition on the 18th of October.

She begins by asking them if they knew what the sign meant that the angel revealed to them. She told them it meant that, "We must make many sacrifices, perform much penance, and visit the Blessed Sacrament [communion] frequently. But first, we must lead good lives. If we do not, a chastisement will befall us. The cup is already filling up and if we do not change, a very great chastisement will come upon us."

After this apparition, the children wrote the message and signed it. All agreed that this was exactly what the Blessed Mother said. The children added, "The Blessed Virgin wants us to do these things, so that we may avoid God's punishment."

The Garabandal apparitions are many. They began in June 1961 and continued until November 1965.

Throughout the recorded experiences and messages, there are prophecies. The first is about this "chastisement." The second is a warning or notice (*el aviso*). And, the third is a miracle, Conchita was the only one to receive the miracle information and is to announce its coming eight days prior to the event.

### The Miracle

By this time, many authorities were asking for a sign, a miracle. When the children asked the Blessed Mother to perform one for the doubters, she turned very grave and stopped smiling. Once, when a tape recorder had been brought to the scene, the children pleaded with Her to speak onto the tape. Just as they were waiting for her to speak, the tape ran out, then an audible voice that everyone heard said, "I will not speak."

The miracle she prophesied is to occur in such a manner that the whole world will know it. Here is how Conchita describes it:

"I am the only one to whom the Blessed Virgin spoke of the miracle. She forbade me to say what it will consist of. I can't announce the date either, not until eight days before it is due to occur. What I can reveal is that it will coincide with an event in the Church and with the feast of a saint, a martyr of the Eucharist; that it will take place at 8:30 on a Thursday evening; that it will be visible to all those who are in the village and surrounding mountains; that the sick who are present will be cured and the doubters will believe. It will be the greatest miracle that Jesus has performed for the world. There won't be the slightest doubt that it comes from God and that it is for the good of mankind. A sign of the miracle (*un senal del milagro*), which it will be possible to film or televise, will remain forever (*para seimpre*) at the pines."

After reading Nostradamus' prophecy of Thursday becoming a Holy Day, Conchita's Thursday miracle is even more curious. Could this miracle be the beginning of a new leader whose Holy Day will be recognized as Thursday because a great miracle occurred on that day at 8:30 p.m.? Certainly, if it is to be "the greatest miracle that Jesus has performed for the world," it's going to be a doozy, deserving of a special Holy Day. I thought raising Lazarus from death was a pretty good miracle. Of course, only a few dozen people saw that one.

When Conchita was asked to explain more about the sign that will remain at the Pines (an area in Garabandal where many apparitions took place), she said:

"The sign that will remain forever at the pines is something that we will be able to photograph, televise and see, but not touch. It will be evident that it is not a thing of this world but from God."

As of yet, Conchita has not gotten the message to alert us eight days before the miracle occurs.

## The Chastisement

Conchita explains the chastisement this way:

"The chastisement is conditional and depends on whether or not mankind heeds the messages of the Blessed Virgin and the miracle. If it should take place, I know what it will consist of because the Blessed Virgin told me about it, but I am not permitted to say what it is.· Moreover, I have seen the chastisement. I can assure you that if it comes, it is worse than being enveloped in fire, worse than having fire above and beneath you. I do not know how much time will elapse between the miracle and the chastisement.

"If we do not change, the chastisement will be terrible in keeping with what we deserve. We saw it, but I cannot say what it consists of because I do not have permission from the Blessed Virgin to do so. I cannot say anything else about the chastisement. When I saw it, I felt a very great fear even though I was looking at the

Blessed Virgin."

A note here: In 1998 the magnetic fields of our planet began to gradually shift. These fields shield us from solar radiation, which is normally channeled to the planet's poles and seen as the Northern and Southern Lights. In 2004 scientists reported that the shifting of these fields could allow solar radiation to penetrate the inhabited areas of the planet and would be a damaging "fire" to the health of humans. You can see this news on a DVD of the PBS TV program produced by Nova titled, "Magnetic Storm."

Interestingly, while the children were viewing the chastisement, many onlookers noticed how terrified they were, and began to pray. As soon as they did so, the children's cries and anguish subsided. But as soon as the onlookers stopped praying, the children immediately went into crying and squirming as though suffering great discomfort.

### The Warning

Conchita wrote that when the world sees the warning, the people would wish that they were dead rather than experience it. She goes on to say:

"The Blessed Virgin told me on the first of January that a warning would be given before the miracle so that the world might amend itself. This warning, like the chastisement, is a very fearful thing for the good as well as for the wicked. It will draw the good closer to God and it will warn the wicked that the end of time is coming and that these are the last warnings. There is more to it than this, but it can't be said by letter. No one can stop it from happening. It is certain, although I know nothing concerning the day or the date."

Along with her statement, Conchita answered specific questions. Of the 18 questions submitted to Conchita on September 14, 1965, four relate to the warning.

Q. Will the warning be a visible thing or an interior thing or both?

A. The warning is a thing that comes directly from God and will be visible throughout the entire world, in whatever place anyone might be.

Q. Will the warning reveal his personal sins to every person in the world and to persons of all faiths, including atheists?

A. Yes, the warning will be like a revelation of our sins, and it will be seen and experienced equally by believers and non-believers and people of any religion whatsoever.

Q. Is it true that the warning will cause many people to remember the dead?

A. The warning is like a purification for the miracle. And it is a sort of a catastrophe. It will make us think of the dead, that is, we would prefer to be dead than to experience the warning.

Q. Will the warning be recognized and accepted by the world as a direct sign from God?

A. Certainly, and for this reason I believe it is impossible that the world could be so hardened as not to change.

Finally, Conchita says that the Blessed Mother told her that there would only be two more Popes after Paul VI! Here are Conchita's own words on this:

"The Blessed Virgin said in 1962 that there will be only two more Popes after Paul VI. But this does not mean that the world will come to an end."

Now we all know the Papal prophecies of Malachy and Nostradamus from a previous chapter. This Garabandal prophecy does not appear to fit with these other prophecies. The Popes during the Garabandal apparitions were John XXIII (1958-63) and then Paul VI (1963-78). Using Conchita's statement, the Pope, John Paul II would then be the last pope. Whereas, Malachy and Nostradamus saw two more popes after John Paul II. We should note here that John Paul II himself felt that it was his destiny to die early in his papacy, but the Holy Mother saved him from death twice, making his reign later than it was originally intended or destined to be. Perhaps there was a shift in the plan from the way it was in 1960s to the 2000s, and perhaps that shift is due to the prayers of the faithful.

Medjugorje, Yugoslavia, 1981

These apparitions began in a similar manner to those in Fatima and Garabandal, though the children are older. A 17-year-old girl sees a luminous silhouette suspended above the ground on a cloud, and calls to her girlfriends, "Look, there's Our Lady, the Blessed Mother." Six children are involved in these apparitions, 2 boys and 4 girls. Most are 16 and 17 years old, but one is only 10. Most of the apparitions occur on or around a mountain, Mt. Podbrodo. As with other apparitions, the children see many wonders, encounter many stern and accusing adults and authorities, but endure to convince many of their sincerity. Onlookers also see miraculous phenomena, which helps to support the belief that something special was happening.

Basically, the luminous lady identifies herself as "The Mother of Peace," and explains:

"I have come to tell the world that God is truth; He exists. True happiness and the fullness of life are in Him. I have come here as the Queen of Peace to tell the world that peace is necessary for the salvation of the world. In God, one finds true joy from which true peace is derived."

At another time she says, "I have come because there are many believers here. I want to be with you to convert and reconcile everyone." She explains:

"You know that I wish to guide you on the way of holiness, but I do not want to force you. I do not want you to be holy by force. I wish every one of you to help yourselves and me by your little sacrifices, so that I can guide you to be more holy, day by day. Therefore, dear children, I do not want to force you to live the messages; but rather, this long time I am with you shows that I love you immeasurably, and that I wish every single one of you to be holy."

## The Chastisement

The Queen of Peace gives the Medjugorje children ten "secrets." The children were told not to reveal the secrets until she gave them permission. It is known that some of the secrets deal with a chastisement that will come to the world. There is some uncertainty about whether this chastisement has already been averted or is yet to come. Apparently, the 7th secret prophesied a chastisement, but the 8th secret said that the chastisement had already been avoided because of world prayer. However, the 9th and 10th secrets each include chastisements. Now, whether these are new chastisements or the same as those mentioned in the 7th secret is unclear to some writers. As I read the material, it appears they are new and different chastisements that are still to come. Perhaps one or both of them correspond with the chastisement the children saw at Garabandal.

Whatever the case, the Queen says that this chastisement can be mitigated "through prayer and fasting." She teaches that the world has lost its understanding of the value of prayer and fasting, and that much can be changed by these practices. She explains:

"Pray with great meditation. Do not look at your watch all the time, but allow yourself to be led by the grace of God. Do not concern yourself too much with the things of this world, but entrust all that in prayer to Our Heavenly Father.... Avoid television ... excessive sports, the unreasonable enjoyment of food and drink, alcohol, tobacco ... Definitely eliminate all anguish. Whoever abandons himself to God does not have room in his heart for anguish." (Anguish usually means extremely distressed, physically or mentally.)

She encourages having "an encounter with God in prayer," a "meeting with God, the Creator." She says, "God gives Himself to you but He wants you to answer in your own freedom to His invitation."

## The Sign

Another secret deals with a sign; a sign left by the Queen that the whole world would see. The children all claim to know when the sign is to occur. The sign is to appear on the apparitional hill. Its presence will be a call for mankind to return to God. "The Virgin said that there would be many more signs throughout the world before the great sign appears." But after the great sign appears, there will be no more time for "conversion." That is why the Virgin calls all to reconcile themselves with God now.

Note here: In the chapter of the cycle of the ages, the next age, an age of enlightenment when all evil is banished from the world for a thousand years, is called the Age of the Lily. It is called this because only the pure of heart may enter during this time. In many of Mary's messages there is a call to get our hearts clear of hatred, earthy desires, regrets, doubts, fears, and anything that holds us down from our more spiritual nature. Here Mary appears to be warning us that there will come a time when no one can convert themselves from their earthy nature to their more spiritual nature, for there will be no more time for such.

## The Warning

Before the visible sign is given, there will come three warnings to the world in the form of singular events on Earth "to allow people to return to God." Once the warnings begin, they will follow in short succession to one another. Enough time will pass between them to allow people to become sufficiently aware of each warning. During this period, many graces will pour out upon the people who seek tuning in to God. This is reminiscent of many biblical prophecies:

Isa. 44:3 For I will pour water on the thirsty land, and streams on the dry ground; I will pour out my Spirit on your offspring, and my blessing on your descendants.

Ezek. 39:29 I will no longer hide my face from them, for I will pour out my Spirit on the house of Israel, declares the Sovereign Lord.

Joel 2:28 And afterward, I will pour out my Spirit on all people. Your sons and daughters will prophesy, your old men will dream dreams, your young men will see visions.

Joel 2:29 Even on my servants, both men and women, I will pour out my Spirit in those days.

Acts 2:17 In the last days, God says, I will pour out my Spirit on all people. Your sons and daughters will prophesy, your young men will see visions, your old men will dream dreams.

Acts 2:18 Even on my servants, both men and women, I will pour out my Spirit in those days, and they will prophesy.

## The Guidance

Throughout the Medjugorje apparitions, the Queen gives much guidance as to what one should be doing in these times. Here are two examples:

"Try to conquer some fault. If your fault is to get angry at everything, try each day to get angry less ... If you cannot stand those who do not please you, try on a given day to speak with them. If your fault is not to be able to stand an arrogant person, you should try to approach that person. If you desire that person to be humble, be humble yourselves. Show that humility is worth more than pride."

"You yourselves know what you have to do. Make a decision for love. Love your neighbors. Love those people from whom the evil is coming to you and so ... you will be able to judge the intentions of the heart. In the power of love you can do even those things that seem impossible to you ... Hatred creates division and does not see anybody or anything. Carry unity and peace. Act with love in the place where you live. Let love always be your only tool. With love turn everything to good."

There is also a universality about the teachings from the Queen of Peace. As in this teaching:

"You must respect each man's beliefs. No one should despise another for his convictions. God is one and invisible. It is not God but it is believers who have caused the dreadful divisions in the world."

Mirjana, one of the six children, tells of being taught by the Lady how devout Roman Catholics go out of their way to avoid contact with Orthodox Catholics and Muslims; yet nobody who refused to take other believers seriously was worthy of the name of Christian." The Lady singled out one of Mirjana's neighbors in Sarajevo, a Muslim woman called Pasha. "She is a true believer, a saintly woman. You should try to be more like her."

As all of us now know, peace did not come to Sarajevo. The dark influences prevailed and the people chose "ethnic cleansing" rather than cooperation, understanding, and love. The Bosnian War was an international armed conflict that took place in Bosnia and Herzegovina between 1992 and 1995. Following a number of violent incidents in early 1992, the war is commonly viewed as having started on 6 April 1992. The war was part of the breakup of Yugoslavia. A total of 13,952 people were killed during the siege of the city of Sarajevo, including 5,434 civilians. The war was fought largely along ethno-religious lines, among predominantly Orthodox Christian Serbs, Muslim Bosniaks, and Catholic Croats. The Dayton peace accord signed in 1995 creates two entities of roughly equal size, one for Bosnian Muslims and Roman Catholic Croats, the other for Orthodox Christian Serbs. An international peacekeeping force continues to oversee the peace.

Today we are witnessing intense stress and conflict among the three main groups of the Children of Abraham: Jews (Israelites, heirs of Abraham's son Isaac and Jacob's name change to *Israel*, meaning "wrestles with God"), and Moslems (Ishmaelites, heirs of Abraham's son Ishmael, meaning "God hears," and the prophet Mohammed, meaning "praiseworthy"), and Christians (an outgrowth of the Jew Jesus of Nazareth, tracing their heritage through David to Abraham). God has made promises to all three but they have and continue to mistrust each other and bring much pain and suffering upon themselves. One has to wonder if the Children of Abraham will ever coexist, let along cooperate.

*** 

The apparitions of the Virgin Mary require some degree of faith on the part of those seeking to understand what it's all about and whether it really is Mary the Mother of Jesus. The parish priest at Lourdes, Father Dominique Peyramale, said, "For those who believe no explanation is necessary. For those who do not believe, no explanation is possible." That's probably true, but I'd like to attempt an explanation, or at least some elaboration.

### The Divine Feminine

The most important element of this is a greater understanding of the entity involved. Who is this entity and what is her role in the big picture?

The Essenes believed that God is both male and female in one, and that the Logos, the essence of being, is Yin and Yang in one. Therefore, to them, there is a Divine Masculine and a Divine Feminine.

The Essenes believed that God meant what He said when He turned to Eve as they were leaving the Garden and prophesied that out of her would come the redeemer of this fall from grace. Therefore, the Essenes were preparing for the coming of the Messiah by looking for the "Eve" that would deliver the "Adam" who would crush the head of the serpent in the Garden of Eden. The Essenes believed the Messiah had to have a feminine component, and God had foreshadowed this in His prophecy in Genesis.

Edgar Cayce's visions explain it this way: There were several females in the Mt. Carmel temple that the Essenes felt to be chosen to fulfill Eve's destiny. One day, a lady named Anne came to their temple. She told them that she was pregnant but had not known any man. This was exactly what they had been looking for! In fact, some in the temple had actually considered Anne to be the female component of the coming of the Messiah. However, when she delivered a female child, some began to believe that even the feminine component had to be immaculately conceived since it was half of the Logos. Mary proved to be just that. While still very young and before she was married to Joseph, she conceived the Holy Child. Here's how Luke records their conversation in his gospel:

"In the sixth month, God sent the angel Gabriel to Nazareth, a town in Galilee, to a virgin pledged to be married to a man named Joseph, a descendant of David. The virgin's name was Mary.

"And coming in to her the angel said, 'Hail O woman richly blessed! The Lord is with you.' Mary was greatly troubled at his words, and kept pondering what manner of greeting this might be.

"But the angel said to her, 'Do not be afraid, Mary, you have found favor with God. Behold, you will conceive in your womb and give birth to a son, and you are to give him the name Jesus. He will be great and will be called the Son of the Most High. The Lord God will give him the throne of his father David, and he will reign over the house of Jacob forever; his kingdom will never end.'

"'How will this be,' Mary asked the angel, 'since I am a virgin?'

"The angel answered, 'The Holy Spirit will come upon you, and the power of the Most High will overshadow you; for that reason the holy one to be born will be called the Son of God. Even Elizabeth, your relative, is going to have a child in her old age, and she who was said to be barren is in her sixth month. For nothing is impossible with God.'

"'Behold, I am the servant of the Lord,' Mary answered. 'May it be done to me as you have said.'

"Then the angel left her." (Luke 1:26-41)

At that time Mary got ready and hurried to a town in the hill country of Judea, where she entered Zechariah's home and greeted Elizabeth. When Elizabeth heard Mary's greeting, the baby leaped in her womb, and Elizabeth was filled with the Holy Spirit. She cried out with a loud voice, "Blessed among women are you, and blessed is the fruit of your womb!"

For the Essenes, the key insight comes in one of the verses that follow these. Elizabeth, filled with the Holy Spirit, speaks the prophecy that the Essenes had held to so faithfully.

"Blessed is she who believed that there would be fulfillment of what had been spoken to her by the Lord." (Luke 1:45)

When was the "fulfillment of what had been spoken to her by the Lord"? To the Essenes, it was when they were leaving the Garden of Eden. Out of Eve would come the redeemer of this fall from grace. In Mary, the Holy Mother, this prophecy was fulfilled.

The Divine Feminine was prophesied to precede the coming of the Divine Masculine, and it did so. Perhaps the Holy Mother's apparitions are in sync with a divine pattern. Perhaps this means that Her son will follow soon.

The ancient Gnostics believed and taught that Wisdom was feminine, and was personified in the goddess Sophia. And in their legends of Sophia, Jesus Christ actually helped her escape from the illusion and darkness of this often deceptive world. Here again we see the blend of Yin and Yang leading to freedom and enlightenment.

Even modern depth psychology has gotten on the feminine-masculine balance, seeing every person having a manifested portion of this yin-yang whole balanced by a subconscious portion. Males are animus (yang) projected with their anima (yin) in their deeper consciousness, and females are anima (yin) projected with their animus (yang) in their subconscious. As a man, I'm to get in touch with my inner feminine and women are to get in touch with their inner masculine.

All of this is coming back into our understanding in these times. But long, long ago these were united. They were not separated until Genesis 2:18-25, though it is written in an unclear and prejudiced manner. The name "adam" in lower case means a person or being, not simply a male. In Genesis *adam* is translated "man" but in the book of Numbers it is translated more accurately as being, or person. Within the *adam* of early creation was the feminine, and it required a "deep sleep" of this androgynous being in order to bring out and separate the feminine, leaving the remaining portion only masculine. If we had only named them Eve and Bob, this would be clear, but they were named Eve and the name for a "being" was simply capitalized, Adam. Now Adam was a male person, but "adam" up to this point was an androgynous being.

Fortunately, we are beginning once again to see the genders as equals of a whole, each with their special features and functions.

Perhaps to his detriment Pope John Paul I wrote about God as Father *and* Mother, which the Church fathers may not have been ready to hear. God is an infinite, eternal spirit in which the dynamics of gender are in oneness and harmony. God is not made in our images as males and females, we are made in God's image, which contains both genders in oneness.

Photograph of an Apparition of Mary on April 2, 1968

# The Great Pyramid Timeline Prophecy
## Pointing Directly to the Year 2038!

The Great Pyramid prophecy also points to these present times. Surprisingly, in the 1800s and early 1900s much of this timeline inside the Great Pyramid was well known and much was written about it. Some of the most important scientists and researchers of that time had detailed knowledge of this timeline and how it correlated with content in the *Egyptian Book of the Dead*. Eventually, points along the timeline were associated with world events, taking it to the level of a prophecy about humankind's journey through material incarnations.

How was this timeline and its prophecy discovered? There were two ways. The first factor dealt with the design of the interior of the Great Pyramid which was unlike anything ever found around the globe in antiquity and would be nearly impossible to recreate today. Therefore, the minds that studied the pyramid's unusual features and amazing craftsmanship knew it had to be more than simply a tomb.

Researcher W. Marsham Adams wrote: "That its various features are meaningless, or the mere result of caprice, is a suggestion to which the forethought and lavishness of the calculation displayed in every detail unmistakably gives the lie. Nor again can we maintain that they are necessary for the purposes of an ordinary tomb. For, they are not to be found in other pyramids which were used for that purpose." (1, p. 34)

Adams' last statement that they were not ordinary tombs is correct, because none of the major pyramids in Egypt contained a mummy – none. The

Great Pyramid and perhaps all of the major Egyptian pyramids, as well as their intricate passageways and chambers were more likely used for active services and ceremonies. Given their apparent association with death, the pyramids may well have been used for death-like initiations, or for preparing select individuals for dying and death and subsequent activity after death.

W. Marsham Adams knew this because in his publication, *The Book of the Master*, quoting from a letter by Sir Gaston Maspero, Adams identifies "the prevalence of a tradition among the priests of Memphis" that "the Secret House [Great Pyramid] was the scene where the neophyte was initiated into the mysteries." (1, p. 179)

Archaeologists concede that no mummy was ever found in any of the major pyramids in Egypt and the sarcophagus in the Great Pyramid never had a lid.

The second factor that contributed to finding the timeline inside the Great Pyramid was the discovery of a measurement associated with the construction of this pyramid. In 1646, John Greaves, professor of astronomy at Oxford, published his Pyramidographia in which he first theorized that the Great Pyramid at Giza was constructed by a geometric cubit, which he called the "Memphis cubit." In 1737, the antiquarian Thomas Birch published research papers based on Greaves' hypothetical cubit. Even Sir Isaac Newton (1642 to 1727) used Greaves' measurements of the Great Pyramid and published them in a paper entitled "A Dissertation upon the Sacred Cubit." In this paper Newton correlated the "Memphis cubit" to the cubit in the Bible. This measurement and its association with the Bible fired up religiously oriented researchers, particularly Christian researchers, who found many correlates between Egyptian theology and Judeo-Christian concepts and stories (i.e., such as an immaculate conception of the

Messiah, Isis conceiving Horus without copulation, and then Horus overcoming Satan, who was Set in Egyptian lore). These researchers began investigating with a more religious view. They were also aided by the translation of the Rosetta Stone (1822), making the *Egyptian Book of the Dead* readable. It wasn't long before the measurement and the esoteric elements of the *Egyptian Book of the Dead* were united. Sir Gaston Maspero (1846-1919), the famous French Egyptologist, professor of archaeology, and developer of the Egyptian Museum in Cairo, explained, "The [Great] pyramid and The Egyptian Book of the Dead reproduce the same original, the one in words, the other in stone." (12, p. 88)

This theory, along with other ideas, became known as Pyramidology. Two essential elements of pyramidology were: (1) that the ancient Egyptian theology and cosmology, both highly moral and spiritual, asserted that human beings were "godlings" formed by the Creator of the entire universe and were destined to return to that condition; and (2) that the amazing construction of the Great Pyramid was done intentionally to preserve a hidden prophecy about these godlings, their journey through evolution, and their ultimate destiny among the stars of the heavens. Judeo-Christian theology—of which most of these early researchers were adherents—considered humans to have been originally created in the image of God (Genesis 1:26-27), and Christians believed that Jesus Christ affirmed human godliness in his statement in the Gospel of John 10:34: "Is it not written in your law, 'I said, you are gods?'" The law he is referring to is found in Psalm 82:6: "You are gods, sons of the Most High, all of you...." Additionally, Egypt had a major role in the Bible stories that most of these researchers accepted as truth. There was even a verse in the Bible that pyramidologists believed was referring to the Great

Pyramid of Giza, Egypt.

Researchers and authors David Davidson and H. Aldersmith published a large book titled, *The Great Pyramid: Its Divine Message* in 1924. In this book the prophecy timeline was meticulously detailed and correlated to known world events and supposed future events. Davidson first got the idea of a timeline from W. Marsham Adams, author of *The House of the Hidden Places: A Clue to the Creed of the Egyptians* (1895) and *The Book of the Master* (1898). Adams wrote that "the unique system of passages and chambers in the Great Pyramid have little meaning as a tomb but have an allegorical significance only explained by referring to the Egyptian Book of the Dead." (12, p. iii) When we think about this, if the Great Pyramid were only a tomb for the pharaoh, it would not need so many passageways, chambers, and unusual features; such as the Great Step, the granite "veil" stone in the antechamber to the King's Chamber, and the distinctive elements of the pyramid's subterranean portion. Adams wrote that select chapters in the Egyptian Book of the Dead refer to an "ideal structure and to the passages and chambers therein, and that these passages and chambers followed precisely the order and description of those of the Great Pyramid."(12, p. 88)

The exact translation of the original title of the *Egyptian Book of the Dead* is, *The Book of Coming Forth into the Light* (often translated *Coming Forth by Day*). And since the Great Pyramid was called Ta Khut, meaning "The Light," you can see how some portions of the papyrus texts might relate to the Great Pyramid, especially since the *Egyptian Book of the Dead* describes passages, halls, chambers, transitions, tests, dangerous or even wrong turns, and various gates through which the dead must make their way—or through which initiates receive training about life beyond death.

Likely influenced by the popular Tibetan Book of the Dead, the German Egyptologist Karl Richards Lepsius, the first translator of the papyrus texts, labeled the whole collection the Egyptian Book of the Dead. Curiously, the *Tibetan Book of the Dead* is actually titled *Bardo Thodol*, which in Tibetan means *liminality liberation*, akin to "threshold of liberation." Its title is often transliterated as *Liberation through Hearing during the Intermediate State*. Both of these books are about consciousness and activity in the Netherworld, or the realm of the dead. However, both appear to also have much information for the incarnate to use in becoming aware of the nonphysical realms of life beyond this physical reality, and may therefore also be useful for experiencing the realms beyond the physical while in physicality. The fact that ancient people were so interested in the life after death of the physical body has added to this theory that the Great Pyramid with its many passageways, chambers, and unusual features may have been used to initiate incarnate souls into the other dimensions of life.

W. Marsham Adams likely got some of his ideas from Professor Charles Piazzi Smyth, Astronomer Royal of Scotland from 1846 to 1888. (Piazzi Smyth was the pioneer of the modern practice of placing telescopes at high altitudes to enjoy the best observing conditions.) Professor Smyth and his wife Jessie (who accompanied him on all of his travels) camped next to the Great Pyramid to measure the exterior and interior of the amazing edifice. Professor Smyth published his book *Our Inheritance in the Great Pyramid* in 1864 and expanded it over the years. This book is also titled in some editions, *The Great Pyramid: Its Secrets and Mysteries Revealed*. Smyth claimed that the measurements he obtained from the Great Pyramid revealed the "pyramid inch," equivalent to 1.001 British inch. He believed it was the standard of measurement used by the architects of the ancient structure. Smyth also believed that the pyramid inch was a divinely inspired measurement handed down from the time of Shem, one of Noah's three sons who are Shem, Ham, and Japheth, and whose descendants eventually became seventy nations (Genesis 10). Shem's descendants became the Semitic populations which include most all Middle Eastern peoples; this would also contain the Jews and Arabs, as well as many others in antiquity. While measuring the pyramid, Smyth wrote that he found the number of inches in the perimeter of the base equal to one thousand times the number of days in a year, and he found a numeric relationship between the height of the pyramid in inches to the distance between Earth and the Sun in miles. He also wrote that "proceeding around the globe due north and due south of the Great Pyramid ... there is more earth and less sea in that meridian than in any other meridian all the equator round." He also wrote that "taking the distribution of land and sea in parallels of latitude, there is more land-surface in the Great Pyramid's general parallel of 30° than in any other." (33, p. 89) And he made attractive and often reprinted maps to support his statements. Unfortunately, when carefully measured, neither of these statements appear to be correct. And there were other pronouncements from various pyramidologists that proved to be incorrect, such as the authoritative statement that the sarcophagus in the King's Chamber and the Ark of the Covenant in the Bible have the same volume—adding a biblical and godly connection between the pyramid and the Bible. Here are the dimensions and volumes of the two famous artifacts. As we can see, the Ark has much less volume than the sarcophagus.

Sarcophagus (interior)—Ark of the Covenant (exterior)
Length = 6.51 feet—Length = 3.75 feet
Width = 2.23 feet—Width = 2.25 feet
Depth = 2.87 feet—Height = 2.25 feet
Volume = 41.67 cubic feet—Volume = 18.98 cubic feet

Thus, the theory that the Great Pyramid contained a prophecy that could be revealed by detailed measurements and correlated with verses in the *Egyptian Book of the Dead* was thrown into doubt as a result of these inaccurate statements by many of the original pyramidologists. Unfortunately, many, many people have repeated these mistaken claims for years, even today.

Nevertheless, before throwing the whole of pyramidology out the window, let's continue with our exploration into the timeline prophecy.

In 1910 while calculating and measuring the prophecy inside the Great Pyramid, David Davidson and H. Aldersmith used a measurement now known as the "pyramid inch," which was derived from John Greaves' original work with the sacred cubit. Subsequent pyramidologists and anti-pyramidologists, such as Petrie, affirmed that the 25-inch sacred cubit was clearly used in the construction of the Great Pyramid.

For David Davidson this use of the sacred cubit in the construction of the edifice was clear evidence that the measuring units did not originate in Egypt and that another more ancient culture using an oral tradition and meeting a cataclysmic end brought the wisdom to Egypt. Here's Davidson: "The fact that these systems were derived from the scale of the Sacred Cubit of 25 P. inches again confirms that the Egyptian units of measure were not formulated in Egypt. The sacred system and its derived Egyptian Units all clearly belong to the period of the former civilization...." (12, p. 70) To support his position Davidson points out that the major ancient cultures all have a legend of a prior culture which met its end in a manner that was devastating. He writes: "In ancient Egypt, the tradition exists as 'The Destruction of Mankind,' in ancient Mexico and Peru as 'The Destruction of the World,' and in Babylonia, and Assyria, and in China, as 'The Deluge.' These traditional accounts, when compared, indicate they are various versions of the Noachian [Noah] Deluge narrative in the Hebrew Book of Genesis." (12, p. 39) Davidson clarifies his comments in a footnote stating, "It must always be remembered, however, that in all stages and periods of civilization the highest forms exist alongside the primitive and barbarous. Even the best authorities permit themselves to forget this." (12, p. 39)

The length of a pyramid inch is not only a portion of the sacred cubit but is also the space on the underside of a stone relief in the antechamber to the King's Chamber, known as the "boss mark".

The boss mark is in the shape of a solar disk setting on the horizon; therefore, the bottom portion of its circle is under the horizon, and the flat bottom of this solar disk is a depth of one "pyramid inch"—the flat space between the base of the slab upon which the boss mark appears and the outer surface of this projected solar disk.

There are critics of this measurement, such as the famous Sir William Flinders Petrie (best known as Flinders Petrie), who wrote in 1883, "This boss on the leaf is very ill-defined, being anything between 4.7 and 5.2 [inches] wide, and between 3.3 and 3.5 high on its outer face." Petrie felt that "this boss, of which so much has been made by theorists, is merely a rough projection, like innumerable others that may be seen; left originally for the purpose of lifting the blocks." (30, 78) Despite Petrie's opinion, the slab and the boss relief are more than a lifting mechanism. The slab is in one of three specialized grooves in the antechamber to the King's Chamber and appears to be the only surviving remnant of what were once three slabs. And the rising solar disk is not likely a lifting device since, as reported by John and Morton Edgar in their expedition from 1904-1909 in "Great Pyramid Passages: Part II, Letters from Egypt and Palestine": "The granite leaf appears to be an inch narrower than its corresponding grooves in the wainscots.... Close examination shows that this difference is made up by narrow one-inch projections or rebates on the north face of the leaf, which make it fit tightly into its grooves. With the exception of these rebates (which are evidence of special design), the whole of the north face of the leaf has been dressed or planed down one inch, in order that one little part in the middle might appear in relief." (13, p. 302) It is an intentional relief, a glyph containing a precise measure-ment for discovering the architects' fundamental measuring unit, as well as the prophecy hidden in the pyramid.

One should also keep in mind that Flinders Petrie's father William (1821–1908, the son of Captain Matthews Flinders, the explorer and cartographer of Australia—its runs in the family) was a pyramidologist! This possibly motivated Flinders to show his father how science and evolution were the better truth and that pyramidology, with its religious and messianic undertones, was a delusion of the religiously inclined. Curiously, many of Flinders' exactingly accurate measurements served to support the themes of pyramidology (using steel tapes and special chains 1200 inches long, Flinders Petrie measured the pyramid with amazing accuracy).

David Davidson believed the pyramid inch measurement (which he also called the "primitive inch") was supported by many more features in, on, and above the Great Pyramid than the boss mark, stating that the obvious connection between a unit of measurement and a chronograph is the astronomical cycles associated with the Great Pyramid's exterior. He writes, "There is the cycle of the Precessions of the Equinoxes, associated in the pyramid's geometry with a standard period of reference of 25,826.54 Solar years. And there is the cycle of the revolution of the Autumnal Equinox from perihelion to perihelion. There is also the cycle defining the variations in the eccentricity of the Earth's orbit." (12, p. 140) He goes on with many more examples of how the pyramid is associated with time and the passage of time.

From passages in the *Egyptian Book of the Dead*, pyramidologists concluded that the pyramid inch not only correlates to a measure of space in the stone structure but also to a measure of prophetic time. The measurement equals one year in time, from the original entrance to the Great Pyramid, through the descending and ascending passageways until reaching the "Great Step" at the top of the Grand Gallery. From that point on, the inch equals one month in time rather than one year. Time speeds up—the same amount of activities happen in one-twelfth of the time they used to take.

According to this model and its biblical connections, the pyramid timeline covers a period beginning with the descent of human souls as "the morning stars" spoken of in the biblical book of Job 38:7 ("When the morning stars sang together, and all the sons of God shouted for joy?") to a resurrection period when all the souls ascend to the heavens from whence they came ("And no one has ascended into heaven, but he that descended out of heaven, even the Son of man, who is in heaven." John 3:13) passing through metaphysical gates, passageways, and chambers of tests and developmental activities. Like this biblical passage of "morning stars," the ancient Egyptians believed that each human had a Star-body and a Star-being deep within him.

The last date in the pyramid timeline is 2038, indicating the end of the prophecy and a major portion of the journey of humankind.

But all of this information—the correlation between the *Egyptian Book of Dead* and features inside the Great Pyramid, the boss mark measuring device, and the prophetic timeline—became entangled with the collection of religious and biblical associations under the banner of *Pyramidology*. Eventually, archaeologists as well as serious researchers divided themselves into two main groups: (1) the scientific group that saw nothing more than ancient remnants of a culture obsessed with surviving death, and in the context of the theory of evolution, these ancient ones had primitive superstitions and mythological tales; and (2) a mystical group of modern researchers who believed that God had a hand in building the Great Pyramid, that the Bible spoke of the Great Pyramid, that the *Egyptian Book of the Dead* was an allegorical record relating to places inside the Great Pyramid, and that the timeline draws a parallel to events in world history and in the future.

They quickly broke into two hard-and-fast positions wherein the scientific group gained the upper hand, and the accepted view of ancient Egypt.

The Scripture that was pointed to most often by pyramidologists was Isaiah 19: 19-20: "In that day there will be an altar to the Lord in the midst of the land of Egypt, and a pillar to the Lord at its border. It will be a sign and a witness to the Lord of hosts in the land of Egypt...." Pyramidologists believe that this passage is speaking of the Great Pyramid when it refers to "an altar to the Lord" and "a pillar to the Lord," but a pyramid is hardly an "altar" or "pillar" and it is not on the border. In his book *A Study in Pyramidology*, Raymond Capt states that the Hebrew word translated as "pillar," *matstsebah*, is "correctly translated *monument*." However, I could find no Hebrew Lexicon that translated *matstsebah* as anything other than a pillar or tree stump.

Extremists on either side of this debate took their points to such a degree that there was no room for reasonable elements of the other side's theories. In the case of pyramidology, the biblical side of this debate often espoused positions that were simply not supportable by any existing evidence. In this case, even good evidence of a prophetic timeline inside the Great Pyramid and a correlation with chapters in the Egyptian Book of the Dead were dismissed along with the rest of the pyramidological theories. Gradually, even reasonable researchers had to leave any part of pyramidology alone, casting it into pseudoscience, or worse, shear fiction. It became taboo. Today, no archaeologists in their right minds would present a paper on the correlation of the Great Pyramid with the Egyptian Book of the Dead—not if they wanted to keep their position at a university, or on an authorized expedition team approved by Islamic Egyptian authorities.

The content in the *Egyptian Book of the Dead* dates to before the pharaohs, the pyramids, and the papyruses (papyri). In remote antiquity the content existed orally. They were called "utterances," only to be spoken as part of a spell-like invocation. They contained "words of power" (hekau). On a coffin lid containing a copy of this ancient content there is written djed-medu, which may be interpreted as "words to be spoken." Even the earliest inscribed texts of the Egyptian Book of the Dead contain portions indicating that they had been composed and revised long before the earliest known pharaohs.

The utterances were first carved on pyramid walls in Saqqara. Scholars agree that the "Pyramid Texts," as they are called, belong to a much earlier people and that priests of the subsequent dynastic periods had received them orally as part of sacred lore. Only later had the words become inscribed on the walls of select pyramids. Of such antiquity were these utterances that the scribes carving the hieroglyphics were perplexed over the origin of the texts and their meaning. [Reported by Gaston Maspero, "La Religion Égyptienne," 1884, in *Revue de l'Histoire des Religions*, t. xii. p. 125.] Yet, the scribes knew these texts were of vital importance and the priests overseeing the inscriptions expressed reverence concerning the texts.

The pyramid texts were first discovered by French Egyptologist Sir Gaston Maspero in 1881. They are found in the pyramid of Unas (Fifth Dynasty; Unas likely ruled from 2375 to 2345 BC, but some date this pyramid to 3333 BC; Unas can also be written Unis). They are also found in the pyramid of Teti (Sixth Dynasty; Teti likely ruled from 2357? to 2332? BC and can also be written as Teta). They are found in the pyramids of Pepi I (2332 to 2283 BC) and Pepi II (2278 BC to 2184 BC) and in the pyramid of Merenra (2260 to 2254 BC). Each of these pyramids is located near the Step Pyramid of Djoser (pronounced zo-ser, dating to the Third Dynasty 2630 BC).

Who were the predynastic people that maintained the oral tradition? They may be those people who built and used the so-called "Egyptian Stonehenge," an assembly of huge stone slabs in the southern Sahara Desert in an area known as Nabta, which dates to about 6,500 years ago! That's 1,000 years before the Stonehenge in England. Since the first Egyptian dynastic period began in 3400 BC with Pharaoh Hsekiu in Lower Egypt (the northern Delta area) and Pharaoh Scorpion I in Upper Egypt (the southern mountainous area), the Nabta people would have been active for roughly 3,000 years before the Egyptian kingdoms. The Dynastic period began in 3400 BC and ended in 525 BC when Egypt was conquered by the Persian Empire, ending the reign of the last Egyptian pharaoh, Ankhkaenre Psamtik III. You may have thought that Cleopatra VII was the last pharaoh of Egypt, but by the time she came along, true Egyptians had been ruled and assimilated by Persians and Greeks for some 500 years.

One last detail about Nabta: We know that this predynastic "Stonehenge" complex once stood on the shoreline of an ancient lake that was formed roughly in 9000 BC when the African monsoon shifted north and tropical rainfall occurred. Then, the African monsoon began to drift to the southwest around 2800 BC, and the desertification that we see today began. Today Egypt is desert on the east, south, and west, except for a little irrigated area along both banks of the Nile River and canals that run off the great river. A high culture capable of building a Stonehenge would have had lush living conditions for nearly 6,000 years, and this would have included the first 1,600 years of the pharaonic dynasties. Interestingly, this means that the Sphinx could have existed in a time of tropical conditions. It would certainly explain the running-water erosion marks on the walls of the Sphinx Pit. But that's another issue—one that we are not getting into here.

The earliest written papyruses of the *Egyptian Book of the Dead* date to between 1580 BC and 1350 BC, which would be the Eighteenth Dynasty—a long time after they were inscribed on early pyramid walls. However, records indicate that written copies existed as early as 2750 BC, but none have been found.

Of course, no one could translate the *Egyptian*

*Book of the Dead* until the discovery of the Rosetta Stone in 1799 by a French soldier, Pierre-François Bouchard, of Napoleon's expeditionary team, and then not until 1822 when Jean-François Champollion's translation of the stone was published. From 1822 on Egyptian hieroglyphs could be deciphered.

Most of the texts in the *Egyptian Book of the Dead* begin with the word *ro* and may be translated as mouth, speech, utterance, spell, enchantment, or incantation. Some archaeologists consider these sections of the *Egyptian Book of the Dead* to be spells cast to guide and protect the soul on his or her journey through the underworld to the heavens. In the first chapters the "deceased" or initiate enters the "tomb," descends into the "underworld," and goes through a series of incantations to awaken its abilities to speak, hear, and move through various passages. These passages are required for his or her successful transition through the realms of the dead – of course, we are speaking of the living dead. The next chapters educate the initiate about the origins of the gods or creative forces and key places. Next are chapters guiding the dead or initiate through the sky in sunlight and in the sun boat, then by night descending again into the underworld to meet Osiris, judge of the souls. Final chapters assert the person's right to be among the citizens of heaven and to be among the gods.

Here is a brief summary of the major sections of the Egyptian Book of the Dead:

Chapters 1-16: The deceased or initiate leaves the "House of the Dead" and enters the tomb. It descends into the underworld. Here the soul body regains its powers of movement without physical muscles and speech without vocal cords.

Chapters 17-63: The mythic origin of the gods and secret places are explained. Then the disembodied deceased or initiate is made to live again in order for it to arise and be reborn with the morning sun—not as physical bodies but as active spirit beings.

Chapters 64-129: The deceased or initiate travels across the sky in the Boat of the Sun as one of the blessed dead. In the evening, the deceased or initiate travels to the underworld to appear before Osiris and have its heart weighed in the balance against the "feather of truth."

Chapters 130-189: Having been acknowledged and vindicated of all accusations, the deceased or initiate assumes power as one of the godlings among the gods. This section also includes assorted chapters on protective amulets, provision of "food," and important places.

As we learned in the previous chapter, in 1924 researchers and authors David Davidson and H. Aldersmith published a large book titled, *The Great Pyramid: Its Divine Message*. In this book the prophecy timeline inside the Great Pyramid was meticulously detailed and correlated to passages in the Egyptian Book of the Dead and then to the known world events and assumed future events.

The Davidson-Aldersmith list of correlations between passageways and chambers in the Great Pyramid and terms and verses in the *Egyptian Book of the Dead* are as follows:

GREAT PYRAMID—EGYPTIAN BOOK OF THE DEAD
Great Pyramid—"The Light" (Ta Khut)
Descending Passageway—"The Descent"
Ascending Passageway and the
Grand Gallery—"Double Hall of Truth"
Entrance to Ascending Passageway—"Door of the Ascent"
Ascending Passageway—"Hall of Truth in Darkness"
Grand Gallery—"Hall of Truth in Light"
Antechamber to King's Chamber—"Chamber of the

Triple Veil"
King's Chamber—"Chamber of Resurrection" &
"Chamber of the Grand Orient" &
"Chamber of the Open Tomb"
Passageway to the Queen's Chamber—"Access to
Chamber of Regeneration"
Queen's Chamber—"Chamber of Regeneration" &
"Chamber of Rebirth" &
"Chamber of the Moon"
Subterranean Chamber—"Chamber of Chaos" &
"Chamber of Upside-Downness" &
"Chamber of Central Fire"
Well Shaft—"Well of Life"
Chambers—"Secret Places of the Hidden God"

This chart looks quite clear, but if one were to read the *Egyptian Book of the Dead* in an effort to find these correlations, one would quickly become perplexed. For example, the "Double Hall of Truth" cannot be found in the *Egyptian Book of the Dead*. One would first have to know that the goddess Ma'at (also Maat) is the goddess of truth, and thus realize that the "Hall of Double Ma'at" is Davidson's Double Hall of Truth. Another example is Davidson's "Chamber of Upside-Downness." It cannot be found in the ancient text. However, the *Egyptian Book of the Dead* does teach how not to walk upside-down in the underworld, which Davidson then correlations to the subterranean chamber. However, in examining Davidson's research more closely, it turns out that he got many of his correlations directly from W. Marsham Adam's book, *The House of the Hidden Places*, and Adam's was not always getting his information directly from the *Egyptian Book of the Dead*. For example, Adam's information about the Queen's Chamber and its correlation with the Second Birth comes from an inscription on the vase of Osur-Ur, which Adams got

102

from Archibald Henry Sayce's (1846-1933) four volumes titled *Records of the Past* (published in 1888 and 1890). (See the Gospel of John 3:3-8 which explains that the First Birth is the birth of the physical being and that the Second Birth is the birth of the spiritual being.) Of course, this does not mean that the information is not valuable and helpful to our study, but it is clearly not coming from the *Egyptian Book of the Dead*; although it is inspired by content in the *Egyptian Book of the Dead*. In this instance we learn from the inscription on the vase that Osiris is the "Second Birth, the Mystery of the Soul, Maker of the gods." We also learn that Osiris' sister Isis is the queen of the Queen's Chamber. It is she who brings the magic of rebirth, as quoted in the *Egyptian Book of the Dead*: "The Osiris [person's name here], whose word is truth, says: 'The blood of Isis, the spells of Isis, the magical powers of Isis, shall make this great one strong, and shall be an amulet of protection [for him against] that would do to him the things which he abominates.'" Utterance 156 (7, p. 43)

The *Egyptian Book of the Dead* is considered to be a guide and a spell-casting protective charm for a discarnate person, in this context it must also be for an incarnate person receiving training about death, the afterlife, and the important "places," challenges, and transitions as one moves from physical activity and consciousness to metaphysical activity and awareness. And since there were no mummies or even evidence of mummies found in any of the major pyramids in Egypt, this idea of training and initiation is not as farfetched as it may first appear. Add to this that even the ancient Egyptians considered it important to know the *Egyptian Book of the Dead* while incarnate, as seen in this passage: "If this text be known upon earth … then will he be able to come forth on any day he please, and to enter into his [afterlife] habitation unobstructed." (Papyrus of Ani) (5, p.

147)

    With the possible exception of the Tibetans and their *Tibetan Book of the Dead* (which was written circa 8 AD, long after ancient Egypt was history), there has been no culture on this planet as interested in and as attentive to the afterlife than the ancient Egyptians—not even hellfire-and-brimstone, fear-generating Christian priests and preachers had as much detail about the afterlife or redemptive tips and techniques for the dead as the Egyptians did.

    Let's examine Davidson's diagram of the Great Pyramid, his measurements, and the relationship of historical events to the timeline prophecy. However, we will do so without Davidson's obvious intention of making all the details fit with Judeo-Christian theology, and by ignoring his description of the Egyptian concepts as "spurious." Piazzi Smyth had a similar attitude toward the master builders of the amazing edifice and the authors of the *Egyptian Book of the Dead*, writing in his *Our Inheritance in the Great Pyramid*, "I have never accused, and do not propose to tax, those profane Egyptians with having had anything to do with the design of the Great pyramid," (33, p. 90). He called them, "Egyptian idolaters" with their "peculiar and alas! degrading religion," [sic] and their "vile hieratic system," (33, p. 6). He did not believe that the Egyptians built the Great Pyramid, proposing that it was designed by God Himself "'to be for a sign and for a witness unto the Lord of Hosts in the land of Egypt,'" (33, p. 596, quoting from Isaiah 19:20).

    It is this type of blatant prejudice that has led modern archaeologists to hold all pyramidology as unworthy of consideration. In more than thirty years of studying ancient Egypt I have found there to be no interest among Egyptologists in even reviewing some of the less controversial elements of pyramidology and the timeline. On one occasion, one of the most famous of Egyptologists living today told me that there was absolutely no reason to consider such "pyramid-idiocy" since it was based in religious prejudice.

Despite all of this, the timeline in the Great Pyramid and the structure of the Great Pyramid show a remarkable correlation to world events, and this data can be obtained only from the pyramidologists. Let's attempt to review Davidson's diagram while overlooking his prejudicial statements and concepts.

We will also ignore Davidson's dash lines, finding them to be his conjectures in an effort to fit dates to Bible stories rather than actual passageways in the edifice, or verses in the *Egyptian Book of the Dead*. Thus, his 4000 BC beginning for the Adamic race is his speculation, not supported by Egyptian texts or stones. We begin with the entrance to the structure.

Use the illustrations on the follow pages to follow along.

In his diagram, Davidson marked the date for the entrance to the Great Pyramid at 2144 BC, and if one were standing at the entrance and imagined its descending passageway to be a telescope looking out to the stars, one would see that it points directly to the polar star. Our planet is not spinning fast enough to maintain a single pole star, thus its natural wobble, like a slow, spinning top, points to different circumpolar stars at different times. The Earth completes one wobble every 25,826.54 solar years, and if you drew a line from the North Pole into space, it would trace out a circle over the course of those 25,826.54 solar years. Walter Cruttenden, director of the Binary Research Institute, an archaeological-astronomical think tank in California, wrote: "Some people called it the Yuga cycle [Hindu], others called it the Grand cycle, and others the Perfect

Year ... But the most common name found in use from ancient Europe to ancient China, was simply the Great Year." (11, pp. xix–xx.) The Great Year is often attributed to Plato's writings and astronomically to the Greek astronomer Hipparchus, who computed the true rate of one complete precession cycle at slightly less than 26,000 years. This cycle is also the time it takes our sun to pass through every constellation (sign) in the Zodiac, moving backward, so our age of Pisces moves into Aquarius, not Aries.

The major circumpolar stars for our planet are Thuban, Kochab, Polaris, Vega, Alrai, and Alderamin. Thuban was the closest star visible with the naked eye to the pole star from 3942 BC until about 1900 BC, when the much brighter Kochab began to approach the pole. Thuban was closest to the pole in 2787 BC, when it was less than two and a half arc-minutes away from the pole. However, as we learned earlier, astronomers have two dates for the pole to shine directly in view from the descending passageway of the Great Pyramid, 3350 BC and 2170 BC. With archaeologists stating that the 2170 BC is simply not the time of the building of the pyramid, it leaves us with the 3350 BC date.

In addition to the Pole Star, Davidson also determined that the "arris edge" of the entrance aligned with the star Alcyone in the Pleiades Constellation (the "Seven Sisters"). The arris edge is an architectural term for the edge formed by the intersection of two surfaces at an angle. In this case, Davidson determined that perpendicular to the arris edges an imaginary line would be pointing to Alcyone in 2644 BC. Why Alcyone? In the myth of Alcyone, "Halcyon Days" are the seven days in winter when storms never occur, indicating peaceful days. This may indicate that the initiation time period, or the deceased's transition time is seven days. But Halcyon Days also means to "harken back to an earlier time" and remember them as idyllic, so this may be the intention of the pyramid builders—remembering human origins are in the heavens, not the earth.

The Pleiades star cluster is one of the most ancient known objects in the heavens. Since they are only 4° off the zodiacal path in the sky, they are easily seen from Earth in the Northern and Southern hemispheres. The Seven Sisters are: Maia, Electra, Alcyone, Taygete, Asterope, Celaeno and Merope. Only six of the seven primary stars are distinctly visible to the naked eye, but the ancients knew of the seventh star. The so-called "lost" star was explained in mythology as Merope deserting her sisters in shame, having taken a mortal husband, Sisyphus, the King of Corinth. Another explanation for the "lost" star is the myth of Electra who was an ancestress of the royal house of Troy. After the destruction of Troy, the grief-stricken Electra abandoned her sisters and was transformed into a comet which became a sign of impending doom. In 2357 BC, Chinese astronomical texts contain reports of "The Blossom Stars," the ancient Chinese name for the Pleiades. In 1000 BC, Hesiod wrote poetically about these stars that were mythologically considered to be daughters of Atlas and Pleione the Oceanid. In his *The Astronomy* he wrote: "The Pleiades . . . whose stars are these – Lovely Teygata, and dark-faced Electra, and Alcyone, and bright Asterope, and Celaeno, and Maia, and Merope, whom glorious Atlas begot ... In the mountains of Cyllene she (Maia, the eldest daughter of the seven Pleiades) bare Hermes, the herald of the gods." (15) And since Hermes is associated with Egyptian Thoth, this becomes significant to our study. In the 700s BC Homer spoke of the Pleiades in his Odyssey and Iliad. There are three direct references to the Pleiades in the Bible: in Job 9:9 and 38:31, and Amos 5:8; and an indirect reference in

Revelation 1:16, which describes a vision of the coming of the Messiah holding seven stars in his right hand. North American Indian tribes have marvelous legends about the seven sisters, and in Hindu tradition Shiva created Kartikeya (also known as Skanda), whose name means: "him of the Pleiades." Obviously, the Pleiades were a significant cluster of stars to the ancient people. And since the ancient Egyptians believed that we all came from the stars and will return to them, it is not surprising that the Pleiades and Alcyone have an association with the entrance to the Great Pyramid.

Let's return to Davidson's diagram.

The entrance has some of the largest stones in the pyramid, forming a corbeled double arch over the entrance. Recall that in 24 BC Strabo wrote, "The Greater [pyramid], a little way up one side, has a stone that may be taken out, which being raised up [*sublato*, meaning to "take up," as in open upward], there is a sloping passage to the foundations [the descending passageway]." The unusual huge double arch and the hidden lifting door are a lot of unnecessary engineering and work, unless they are intended to convey more than a simple entrance. Which may be the case, for just below the double arch is the hieroglyph for the "horizon," indicating that this entrance is the "horizon of the Light" (Ta Khut, meaning "the Light," which was the Egyptian name for the Great Pyramid).

The Egyptian legend of the descent of the metaphysical godlings of the Creator out of the realms of the stars and into the depths and density of matter is represented by the descending passageway leading from the entrance to the subterranean "Pit" in the bedrock beneath the Great Pyramid's structure (another amazing and seemingly unnecessary feature of design and construction unless it has meaning beyond a tomb). Davidson saw and wrote that the starlight shining down this descending passageway "symbolized the promise of ascent even whilst descent was taking place."

Using the guideline that the pyramid inch equals one year of time until reaching the Great Step when the pyramid inch equals one month, Davidson measured the passageways throughout the Great Pyramid, correlating his findings with the Bible stories. As we can see, he considered the date for the Exodus of Israelites out of Egypt and onto the Promised Land to correspond with the first ascending passageway.

In the *Egyptian Book of the Dead* there are many gates that must be passed. Davidson associates the entrance to the first ascending passageway with the Gate of the Ascent.

As we have learned, Davidson translated "The Hall of Double Ma'at" (also spelled Maat, goddess of truth) as "the double halls of truth." The first hall is the first ascending passageway, which Davidson called "Hall of Truth in Darkness," and considered to be Israel under the yoke of the Law of Moses and the long journey through the desert to the Promised Land. The passageway is so low that an initiate would have to bend over, possibly even duck-walk, in order to progress through this small but long passageway. As we can see in the diagram, Davidson's measurements reveal that the last step in the Hall of Truth in Darkness is dated to 4 BC, which he concluded must be the correct date for the birth of the Messiah Jesus. Davidson couldn't have known that roughly a century later researchers would uncover the edict issued by King Herod to kill all male children two years of age and younger in an effort to kill the newborn Jesus; and that it was dated by scholars to 4 BC.

One's head clears the low passageway at the date of 30 1/4 AD, which Davidson assumed was the actual date of the crucifixion. Davidson identified this point with the passion of the Messiah. Egypt's Messiah was Horus, immaculately born of Isis, who conceived the child messiah with the help of Thoth's stirring, and awaking her godly, limitless, life-giving powers. She and Horus suffered many trials brought on by the Egyptian Satan: Set. Set and the grown Horus eventually become the two combatants in the battle of the dark and the light in the *Egyptian Book of the Dead*.

Here we arrive at the passageway to the Queen's Chamber, which Davidson titled "Chamber of Second Birth" or "New Birth" and associated with the resurrection of Jesus and his teaching to Nicodemus about the need to be born a second time: "'Truly, I say to you, unless one is born anew, he cannot see the kingdom of God.' Nicodemus said to him, 'How can a man be born when he is old? Can he enter a second time into his mother's womb and be born?' Jesus answered, 'Truly, I say to you, unless one is born of water and the Spirit, he cannot enter the kingdom of God. That which is born of the flesh is flesh, and that which is born of the Spirit is spirit. Do not marvel that I said to you, "You must be born anew." The wind blows where it wills, and you hear the sound of it, but you do not know from whence it comes or whither it goes; so it is with everyone who is born of the Spirit.'" (John 3:4-8 RSV)

The second ascending passageway is the Grand Galley, which Davidson called "Hall of Truth in Light." He wrote that the first hall is passed while one is still uncertain about Divine guidance and one's relationship to God—as indicated by the Israelites building a golden calf to represent their god, then later destroying the calf and accepting an unseen God and His Ten Commandments as a covenant between God and the people. The second hall is the hall of truth through which one passes while possessing some enlightenment about the Divinity and one's relationship to the unseen

God.

The Grand Gallery is just that, grand! When one finally makes it out of the first low ascending passageway, having struggled to ascend it in a bent-over position, and then stands up fully to see the next passageway, its grandeur is awe inspiring, even though it is another rising passage 153.1 feet long. It has seven corbelled walls ascending 28 feet above floor; each slab of wall is outset from the other by three inches. One is standing on a floor that is 6.8 feet wide, with the walls sloping inward to a high narrow ceiling that is only 3.4 feet wide, adding to the wonder of the magnificent hall. High up at the end of this upward sloping Grand Gallery is the Great Step, which is three feet high. Then there is another low passageway into the "Chamber of the Triple Veil," which subsequently leads into the King's Chamber.

As we saw earlier, the pyramid inch was derived from the sacred cubit of 25 inches and the measurement under the boss mark. Throughout the pyramid this inch is equivalent to one year of time, and Davidson uses this data. However, once we reach the floor to the King's Chamber, one pyramid inch is equivalent to one month. Time is twelve times faster than it has been. And we see this in Davidson's diagram.

Many, many researchers and writers have assumed that the Chamber of the Triple Veil was a portcullis, which is a strong, heavy stone sliding up and down in vertical grooves; when lowered it blocks a gateway to a fortress or town, or in this case the King's Chamber. Portcullis comes from the French *porte coulissante*, meaning "gliding door." However, some of the researchers who took a closer look at this strange chamber have concluded that it was not a portcullis. The Edgar brothers are among these, writing: "...when, however, we begin to investigate the subject more closely... we find that there are distinctive peculiarities about the 'granite leaf' [this is the one with the boss mark], which make it certain that it, at all events, had not been intended by the architect to serve as a portcullis [a blocking stone]." (14, p. 488)

On the other hand, J. P. Lepre spent fifteen years in the 1970s and '80s investigating the pyramids of Egypt, focusing on the Great Pyramid, and he found the other four fractured granite stones and matched them to the grooves in the Chamber of the Triple Veil, giving much evidence that this was indeed a portcullis, that could block passage to the King's Chamber when the stones were lowered.

As to the timeline, each lower passage is a time of hardship in the world. In Davidson's diagram (see illustrations) the first low passage is the time of "the war to end all wars," World War I (1914-1918). Recall that in Fatima, Portugal, on October 13, 1917 Mary, the mother of Jesus, appeared to three children and prophesied the end of WWI but foretold that an even greater war was coming, World War II. But she also told the children to pray hard for the souls and church in Russia because within days atheism would take control. Bolshevik-Soviet Revolution began with the takeover of government buildings on October 24, 1917, known as "Red October," and atheistic communism took over Russia. In 1922 the *Bezbozhnik* magazine (literally, "The Godless" magazine) was publishing anti-religious articles. State atheism in the Soviet Union was known as *gosateizm* and was based on the ideology of Marxism-Leninism. Lenin was the founder of the Soviet state and wrote the infamous line: "Religion is the opium of the people." The new Soviet state expropriated all church property, including the churches themselves, and in the period from 1922 to 1926, twenty-eight Russian Orthodox bishops and more than 1,200 priests were murdered, and a much greater number were subjected to persecution. When we consider how much of the ancient Egyptian attention was devoted to spirituality, especially as related to the *Egyptian Book of the Dead* and the Great Pyramid, it is more likely that this low passage (always an indication of hardship and effort) relates more to the spiritual loss than the socio-economic one.

Once through the Chamber of the Triple Veil we must bend again for another low and longer passageway. The second low passage begins with the early stages of the Great Depression (1929-1939) and its devastating effects in virtually every country on the planet and every socio-economic stratum from rich to poor. The Great Depression ended with the start of World War II (1939-1945), and the war ended in the middle of the King's Chamber, or the Chamber of the Open Tomb (1945).

Interestingly, in this Chamber of the Open Tomb, Lepre discovered a stone in the west wall of the Chamber that does not fit the positioning of all the others in this room. He surmised that this could indeed be a *removable* stone revealing another passage-way or chamber. To this date, no one has attempted to move the stone and investigate.

Davidson's timeline ends in 1953 when it reaches the south wall of the King's Chamber. Davidson was sure the End Times were upon us and the "Judgment of All Nations" (as he called it) would begin. However, from Edgar Cayce's visions we learn that Davidson was supposed to go up the wall to the apex above the Chamber of the Open Tomb and its so-called "relieving stones."

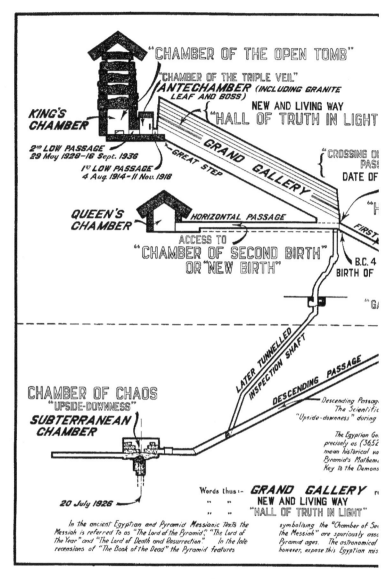

David Davidson's Diagram – the names in gray outline type are names from *Egyptian the Book of the Dead*.

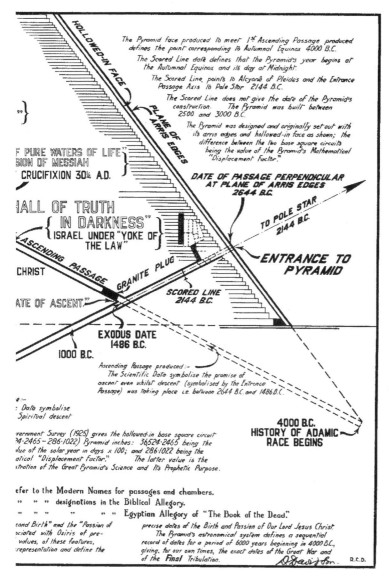

The Pyramid face produced to meet 1st Ascending Passage produced defines the point corresponding to Autumnal Equinox 4000 B.C.

The Scored Line date defines that the Pyramid's year begins at the Autumnal Equinox and its day at Midnight.

The Scored Line points to Alcyoné of Pleides and the Entrance Passage Axis to Pole Star 2144 B.C.

The Scored Line does not give the date of the Pyramid's construction. The Pyramid was built between 2500 and 3000 B.C.

The Pyramid was designed and originally set out with its arris edges and hollowed-in face as shown; the difference between the two base square circuits being the value of the Pyramid's Mathematical "Displacement Factor."

HOLLOWED-IN FACE

PLANE OF ARRIS EDGES

F PURE WATERS OF LIFE"
SION OF MESSIAH

CRUCIFIXION 30¼ A.D.

DATE OF PASSAGE PERPENDICULAR AT PLANE OF ARRIS EDGES 2644 B.C.

TO POLE STAR 2144 B.C.

IALL OF TRUTH
IN DARKNESS"
ISRAEL UNDER "YOKE OF THE LAW"

ASCENDING PASSAGE

CHRIST

GRANITE PLUG

ENTRANCE TO PYRAMID

ATE OF ASCENT"

SCORED LINE 2144 B.C.

1000 B.C.

EXODUS DATE 1486 B.C.

Ascending Passage produced :—
The Scientific Data symbolise the promise of ascent even whilst descent (symbolised by the Entrance Passage) was taking place i.e. between 2644 B.C. and 1486 B.C.

e :—
: Data symbolise
Spiritual descent

4000 B.C.
HISTORY OF ADAMIC RACE BEGINS

vernment Survey (1925) gives the hollowed-in base square circuit ⁴4·2465 – 286·1022) Pyramid inches: 36524·2465 being the due of the solar year in days x 100; and 286·1022 being the atical "Displacement Factor." The latter value is the stration of the Great Pyramid's Science and its Prophetic Purpose.

efer to the Modern Names for passages and chambers.
"   "   " designations in the Biblical Allegory.
"   "   "   "   " Egyptian Allegory of "The Book of the Dead."

cand Birth" and the "Passion of
sciated with Osiris of pre-
values, of these features,
representation and define the

precise dates of the Birth and Passion of Our Lord Jesus Christ.
The Pyramid's astronomical system defines a sequential record of dates for a period of 6000 years beginning in 4000 B.C., giving, for our own Times, the exact dates of the Great War and of the Final Tribulation.

D Davidson.     R.C.D.

David Davidson's Diagram – the names in black type are names used today.

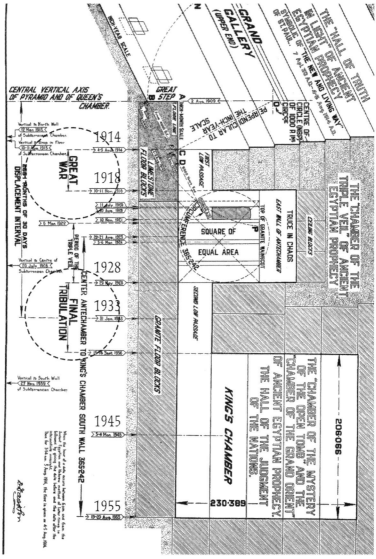

David Davidson's Diagram – from the "Great Step" through the "Chamber of the Triple Veil" and into the King's Chamber. With the dates for WWI, the Great Depression, WWII, and the End of Time – which Davidson thought to be 1955, but Cayce directed us up the wall to the 7 Stones above, the 7 Stages to 2038.

## Pyramid Prophecy Timeline

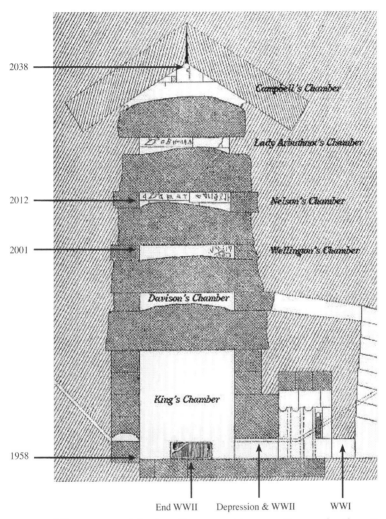

2038

2012

2001

1958

Campbell's Chamber

Lady Arbuthnot's Chamber

Nelson's Chamber

Wellington's Chamber

Davison's Chamber

King's Chamber

End WWII     Depression & WWII     WWI

The pyramid timeline continues through the 5 granite stones to the 2 mitered limestone blocks forming the vaulted ceiling at the top of the chamber's complete structure. If we continue measuring this, the prophetic timeline actually ends at the apex in the year 2038.

## The Seven Ages of Humanity

"We give the secret wisdom of God, which He has kept
in hidden since before the world came into existence."
(I Corinthians 2:6-8, BBE)

Now here is a very strange tale found in ancient
lore. It is a tale about heavenly beings who got their
celestial minds trapped in a lower dimension, a
dimension of form and confining material substance.
Initially only a small group got trapped, mostly due to
their curiosity, which we all know from the classic
proverb *killed the cat*. Upon seeing that the group had
lost their celestial freedom and were now trapped in
matter, a second group entered the physical dimension
to save the first group the first group. Ah but they got
trapped too. A third group, known as "the Elect,"
perceived that there was something very captivating
about physical life, so they decided to setup seven
stages that would get every celestial being in, through,
and out of this dimension, and back to their proper,
immortal, celestial realms. These are the seven ages of
humanity – humanity being the Children of God who
got lost in a lower dimension despite being made in the
image of their Creator, an image that was spirit and
consciousness, not matter.

A twist on this tale is that the first group were
actually the so-called "Fallen Angels" who disobeyed
God's instructions, and thereby found themselves out of
the heavenly realms.

The Maya, Aztec, Toltec, Inca, Hopi, Navajo, and
other American peoples have detailed legends about the
ages of humanity. They each have different names for
these "Ages" – the "Suns," the "Worlds," the "Stages,"
and the like – but their legends are similar.

The First Age was not as physical as we have

today. People and places existed in thought. The Navajo explain that all was the mental "conception" of being, but all had not yet become such in matter, in physical form. Even though all was simply in its essence, its spirit, this First Age was an age of power and might, but also of darkness and chaos. As in the biblical Genesis, a spirit of negativity arose in the initially pure goodness of Creation. This spirit went against the normal order of the Creation, causing much strife and unhappiness. In some of the legends, the forces of life destroyed the first age; in others, the good people sought a better world, a better place, and journeyed to find the Second World, or Second Age, often referred to as the Second Creation. But such stress and striving caused the created Children of God to take on more self-centeredness, more form and substance, making them heavier and more earthy. To help with this the Forces of Life gave them a "firmament," upon which they could catch a vision of the greater whole of creation and levels of consciousness: above, between, and below; or heaven, earth, and the underworld. This is often symbolized in the classic Tree of Life, with its roots in the underworld, its trunk in the material world, and its branches and leaves in the heavens.

The Third Age began as humanity sought to improve. The plan for the Third Age was to "plant and grow," to become the best one could be. In this Age the most perfect "Blue Maze people" were created according to the Maya, with bodies that helped them more fully incase their spirit. But difficulties persisted, and a vane spirit appeared among the created, causing them to fight against one another, become jealous of one another. That spirit even caused them to eventually hate others that they confusingly saw as no longer a part of the initial soul group. The created had power and free will, and many misused them. Many others became saddened and sought a new place, a new era, another age in which to recover what was being lost.

In the Fourth Age all the magic and power we possessed in prior ages was lost. Humanity became a being among the animals, with only their wits to guide them. Now humanity was in solid, physical form, using a body akin to that of the Simians (great apes). In this Age, we were truly terrestrial beings, losing much of our celestial nature and knowledge. Worse yet, we were now caught in the evolution of matter.

But in the human heart of many still burned the desire to become the best we could be, so in the Fifth Age – the "Age of Movement" according to the Maya, and, the "first age of sunlight" according to the Navajo – we began to rise upward, with many tests along the way, tests to see if we had learned how to use power and free will in harmony with the Forces of Life.

The Aztec sun disk appears to end with the Fifth Age, but the final two ages are hidden in symbols of two pyramids. Secretly the legends tell of two more Ages to come. The first is the Age of "the spirits of living things," a time when we regain our awareness of the true essence of life forms and their cosmic, celestial nature. This is akin to the Gnostic consciousness called, "the Fullness of Being." As difficult as it may be to believe, we are now living in this age! But we must be in the earliest stages of this age because things don't seem so great – certainly not as great as we would expect.

The final Age is called by the Navajo "The Place of Melting into One." In this "last" Age (totaling Seven Ages), all life regains its sense of oneness and reunites with the original single source out of which all came into being.

### The Aztec Four Ages within a Fifth plus 2 More

In Nahua (Aztec and Toltec), Maya, Mixtec, Zapotec, and Otomi legends there are normally four creations, "world ages," or "suns." We find the same number among the Navaho and Pueblo of North America and the Quechua in Peru. The age we currently live in is the fifth world age and is the sum of the previous four ages, resulting in the concept of five in four, as carved in the magnificent Aztec Sun Stone (see illustration). This Sun Stone is currently on exhibit in the National Museum of Anthropology in Mexico City. It is a 25-ton, basalt, circular monolith, almost 12 feet in diameter. The Aztecs called it the *Cuauhxicalli* or "Eagle Bowl." It illustrates both mythological and astronomical messages. On this magnificent stone the sign that names the present "sun" or age, called *Movement* (*Nahui Olin*), is composed of the signs that name the previous four suns or ages which, interestingly, correspond to the four elements (earth, water, fire, and air). The order of these ages is in question and varies from record-to-record, but the Akasha would dictate that these go in clockwise order around the Sun Stone beginning in the upper right. Therefore, the order of the suns or ages is: 1) Jaguar Age (*Nahui Ocelot* – earth), 2) Water Age (*Nahui Atl* – water), 3) Fiery Rain Age (*Nahui Quiahuitl* – fire), and 4) Wind Age (*Nahui Ehecatl* – air). In each age humans assumed a different form: In the first age they were giants whose hearts became like wood; in the second, like fish; in the third, like birds; and in the fourth, like apes.

The fifth age is indicated in the very center of the circle by the face of the Sun god (*Tonatiuh*) and the age of *movement* or change. The Mayan calendar indicates that the fifth age *ended* December 21-23, 2012. After the fifth age the legend has two final ages, the last of which returns humanity to its oneness with their Creator and the celestial, heavenly dimensions of life. These two ages are indicated by two small pyramids on top of the circle, one is stripped, which is the sixth age, and one is solid, which is the final seventh age of the long journey.

These ages are enclosed by two huge serpents encompassing the outer rim, meeting at the bottom of the circle. Out of the mouths of the two serpents appear the face of the Sun god (right serpent) and the Fire god (left serpent). The four points of compass directions (north, east, south, and west) and the four seasons of the year (spring, summer, fall, and winter) – similar designs can be found in other ancient cultures, showing the ages, zodiac, seasons, and compass points.

When we combine the Aztec and Maya versions of the creation story through the four ages or suns, we have the following.

*It is helpful to read these as metaphorical, as one would interpret a dream and its symbolism.*

**1st. The Age of Jaguar** (Element: Earth)

In the Jaguar Age the people were giants, with great power, but became like wood. The wooden people were stiff-necked and heartless, no longer listening to the gods and not seeking the light of the gods. Therefore, the gods caused the light of the sun to be eclipsed, and in the resulting darkness jaguars and other beasts of the world ate up the wooden people. So repulsive were the wooden people that even things like grinding stones and cooking pans attacked them, saying: "We have been shattered by you every day, every day, night and day, all the time; crunch, crunch, scrape, scrape, on our faces you went." This same tale is found in the Quechua myth from Peru but with slightly different animals.

Seeing this terrible situation, the Wise Mind became the morning and evening star, Venus. Its illumination would reduce the darkness of the Jaguar Age. To soften the darkness, Wise Mind, as Venus, heralds the coming of the Sun in the morning for 260 days and lingers after the setting Sun in the evening for

260 days. In Genesis 1:14-15, we find a correlating reference to this, "And God said, Let there be lights in the firmament of heaven to divide the day from the night; and let them be for signs, and for seasons, and for days and years; and let them be for lights in the firmament of heaven to give light upon the earth, and it was so." This extra light, and the other lights of the night (the moon and stars) cured the curse of the Jaguar Age.

**2nd. The Age of Water** (Element: water)

In the Age of Water the people were made of mud (Aztec) or clay (Maya). They were created to be conscious, aware of the thirteen heavens, nine levels of earth, and nine realms of the underworld, and to nourish the gods (symbolic of the godly portion of themselves) with prayers and offerings. However, the people lost their consciousness, blending so completely into the watery world that they turned into fish. This was unacceptable; they were to be fully conscious celestial souls, not fish lost in one dimension of life. This is not literal but, like a dream, it is the imagery and symbolism of the deeper levels of the mind. The story is trying to convey the essence of an event that was only barely physical yet so important to gaining an understanding of our origins. The water represents a less dense aspect of matter into which the descending godlings moved. Once in it they so merged with it that they became lost. For all intents and purposes, they were like fish in the sea, unaware of the worlds beyond the water. The Mayan *Popol Vuh* talks about this being a time of the creation of animals, who could not praise and worship the gods because they could not speak: "They just squawked, they just chattered, they just howled. It wasn't apparent what language they spoke, each one gave a different cry." For the companions of the Creator of the cosmos, this was an intolerable condition and could not be allowed to go on eternally. It was truly a Tower of Babel. Cayce's visions teach that prior to this deep descent into self-centeredness and matter, the Children of God all spoke one language, and understood each other – however far away they were from one another.

In an attempt to correct this confusion, the celestial water merged with the waters below to create a great flood that cleansed the world of fish-like people. But the flood made things worse. Wise Mind saw that the horizon was lost due to the flood waters, and because of this no one could determine in which direction to go, or from which direction they came. Therefore, Wise Mind separated the waters above from the waters below by becoming the planet Venus, the planet of loving vibrations and intentions. The legend says that Venus "wounds the sources of water," keeping the rain-gods from bringing the flood again. Now the waters above are separated from the waters below. This same tale is recorded in Genesis 1:6-8, "And God said, Let there be a firmament in the midst of the waters, and let it divide the waters from the waters. And God made the firmament, and divided the waters which were under the firmament from the waters which were above the firmament: and it was so. And God called the firmament Heaven. And there was evening and there was morning, a second day."

**3rd. The Age of Fiery Rain** (Element: fire)
In the third age people are made like birds. Initially they were great eagles, flying high and seeing far! But as the age continued they became more like turkeys than high-flying eagles. They could only walk on the earth and fly a little ways off the ground. In the *Popol Vuh* this age ultimately causes our Heavenly Twins (Sun and Venus) to determine that the Earth will never be an inhabitable place until evil and darkness are defeated, and they decide to enter the Underworld and defeat darkness and

the Lords of Darkness, the forces of evil. *Xibalba* is the legendary underworld or netherworld for the Maya, *Mictlan* for the Aztecs. As I've indicated earlier, it is *representative*; a metaphor for the unenlightened mind where all manner of darkness and death abide. It is considered by the Maya to be a "watery place." In the legend of the Heavenly twins warriors – first the Maize God Twins and then the Hero Twins – they go into the Underworld and there they experience many trials, tests, and challenges. They die from their mistakes and weaknesses, but each time they rise from their ashes again and again. They continue to face every challenge that is brought against them by the Dark Lords of the Underworld, representing the forces within the minds of the godlings, the Children of God, who are struggling with the challenges of independent consciousness and free will. Ultimately, they subdue the forces of evil and darkness, taking away the power of the lords of darkness, death, and evil. Now the Earth is finally ready for a more perfect creation: the Blue Maize People! This portion of the Mesoamerican creation story corresponds almost exactly to the Akasha's creation story of the first Eden in Atlantis – where initially beautiful, powerful, creative people eventually lose their way, and cause destruction to their world, ending the so-called First Creation (as recorded in Genesis 6).

In the *Popol Vuh* "Wise Mind" created blue maize people from yellow and white maize (corn) with the help of the goddess Xmucane (Maya, pronounced *she-mu-cane*) or Cihuacoatl (Aztec: literally, *woman serpent*, and pronounced *see–who-ah–coat-el*). In this story the corn is identified with the bones of the fish people, which Wise Mind retrieved from the Underworld. The serpent goddess Xmucane grinds the bones or corn into meal that she then places in a sacred bowl, around which the gods gather and shed drops of their blood in order to turn the meal into a substance that can make a physical body for the spirit-children to use. These blue maize people are god-like, able to see visions, read thoughts, perceive the secrets of the four world-ages and know instantaneously what is happening anywhere in space. Wise Mind and the Heart of Heaven realize that these maize people are too perfect and will establish an eternal home in materiality on the Earth, never seeking the Heavens again. In order to preserve the Heavens as the true realm and the godlings as the true nature of humanity, the gods decide to "chip the eyes of the maize people," causing them to lose some of their vision and thereby deprive them of establishing an eternal kingdom on Earth. This loss of vision humbled the maize people. Now they needed to seek deeper understanding, to seek the light of truth in their darkness. Powerful beings who lose power is a theme found in many ancient legends; even the Bible recounts that "The Nephilim were in the earth in those days" and God repented having created them. (Genesis 6:1-4)

To compensate for this loss of vision and power, the gods create beautiful wives for the maize people. This corresponds with the creation of the feminine and the Atlantean story of the creation of Lilith.

In their darkness, the first tribes of the maize people journey to the place of the Seven Caves and Seven Canyons (*Tulan Zuiva*) – a possible metaphor for entering the temple of the physical body with its seven hidden chakras and lotuses. There they received their patron gods, including Tohil, a patron god of the Quiché and the source of fire, the element of this age. When the people finally leave the Seven Canyons, they no longer speak one language and now travel in five different groups and directions, exactly as the Akasha describes the original five races, five nations, and five senses separating and going to specific locations on the Earth.

This was not a punishment, but a decision to help shorten the time it takes for the godlings to recover their Heavenly nature and awareness. By dividing in five groups, each focusing on one of the five senses and mastering it, they all gain by this division of labor.

### 4th. The Age of Wind (Element: air)

The symbol for the fourth age is a stylized turkey, indicating that the godlings are still weak and earthbound. The fourth age was the age of the Wind with its hurricane, when people became like apes, simians. It would be an age of strong winds against which the people would have to hold on tightly. Therefore, their hands were made for powerful gripping, hence the prehensile thumb. Rather quickly the age proves no better than the three before it because the godlings continue to lose their way in this physical world with selfish desires. It ends by devastating hurricanes, tornadoes, and wind storms. Once everything is swept away, the four ages are ready for the process of more dramatic, faster change, and the fifth age begins.

### 5th. The Age of Movement

For the Aztecs, this age begins in the city of Teotihuacan, literally "the place of those who would become gods," considered the place where time began. Here the gods came together in a great meeting to determine who would be the new sun to light the new age. They are faced with two choices, represented by two gods who volunteer for the mission: *Tecuciztecatl* and *Nanahuatzin*. The first god is showy, proud, and offers the finest raiments of quetzal plumes and golden balls, with awls of jade tipped with red coral, and incense of the rarest fragrance. The second god is sickly, and offers bundles of reeds, maguey spines dipped in his own blood, and for incense burns scabs picked from his body. The gods prepare a great fire to test which of these two choices will make the best sun.

The Aztec Sun Stone *Cuauhxicalli*, "Eagle Bowl."

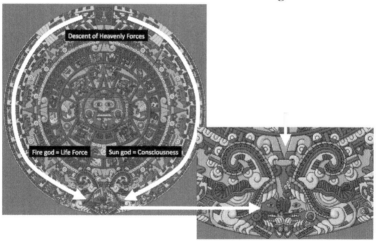

Two serpents encompass the scene, meeting at the bottom. Out of the mouths of the serpents appear the face of the Sun god (right) and the Fire god (left). They symbolize *consciousness* (Sun, "the Light") and the *élan vital*, the life force within us (Fire) – which is the kundalini of the *Yoga Sutras*. They are Mind and Energy.

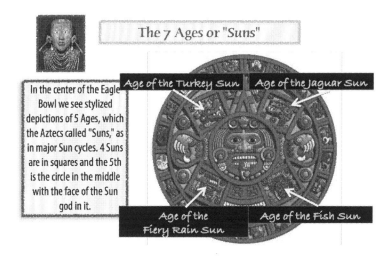

The Four "Suns" or Ages.

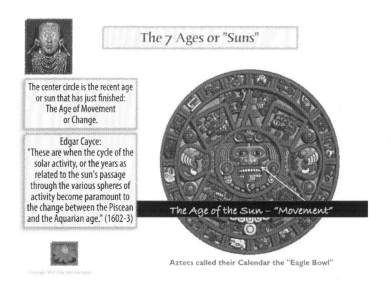

The Fifth "Sun," or Age: *The Age of Change.*
It ended December 21-23, 2012.

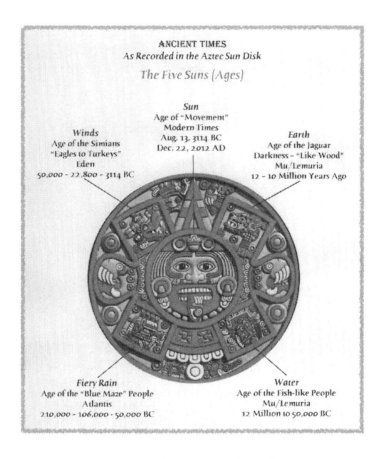

Dates using Mayan dates *and* Edgar Cayce's ancient timeline of events – which includes the legendary lands of Lemuria in the Pacific Ocean and Atlantis in the Atlantic Ocean. There were two Edens, first in Posidea, Atlantis and the second in modern-day Iraq between the classic rivers, Tigris (biblically called *Hiddekel*) and Euphrates. (Genesis 2:8-15)

ANCIENT TIMES
*As Recorded in the Navajo Legends*

The Seven Suns (Ages)
Last Two Ages

*The Sixth Age - "The Spirits of Living Things"*
This follows the Age of Movement with the return of Spirit-Awareness

*The Seventh Age - "The Place of Melting into One"*
The Return to original Oneness

The Two Pyramids symbolizing the Last Two Ages:
the Age of the "Spirit of All Living Things" and the Age
of "Melding Back into Oneness."
We have entered the Sixth Age!

— continuing the Fifth Age from page 127:

As the test proceeds, it turns out that the showy choice cannot withstand the heat of the fire and retreats; but the second lowly choice jumps straight into the white-hot fire and is consumed immediately. So taken by the bravery of this act, the retreating showy god returns and follows the lowly one into the fire. So taken by these brave acts all the godlings, those that are the eagles and that are the jaguars, also jump into the fire. The company of gods waits to see where these gods will reappear. Slowly the sky reddens and the new sun appears, red hot in the eastern sky. Shortly thereafter the moon also appears in the eastern sky. Worried that the two lights will make the Earth too bright, the gods dim the moon's light. Then all the stars appear in the night sky to keep the light on when the sun is away.

These two choices are symbolic of the way of self-glorification, self-exaltation versus humility, meekness, and sacrifice. It is decided that the latter will guide all people to the deeper truth and higher achievements. It is the bright, life-giving light of the sun. Whereas, the self-exaltation is the dimmer moon light. This tale is reflected in modern astrology where the sun is your true self and the moon is your personality.

In the Aztec tale, the new sun and moon are stationary in the sky. This isn't good because it does not reflect the cycles of growth through trials, tests, failures and resurrections. All the gods have come to know these requirements to overcome their being lost in darkness, death, and evil. *Movement* must begin. But, the new sun (now called, *Tanotiuh*) demands that the company of the gods shed their blood also, before movement begins. He insists that all must help this great effort. After initial resistance, the gods finally comply with the sun's demand and begin to put their hearts into a sacred fire for resurrection, and in the long, trying journey of life through selfishness. One by one Wise Mind cuts the hearts out of each god with a sacred knife. From this legend one finds the source of the distorted understanding that led many ancient Mesoamerican priests into the brutal, bloody practice of cutting hearts out of human bodies. They had lost so much wisdom to the higher, finer understanding that they could no longer perceive the metaphorical meaning behind the legends. The symbolism of this heart-removing act among the godlings matches the Old Testament teaching of circumcising their hearts so they are more compatible with the Heart of Heaven of God. Here are a few examples:

"Circumcise therefore the foreskin of your heart, and be no more stiff-necked." (Deuteronomy 10:16) This is reminiscent of the "wooden people" in the Jaguar Age who became stiff-necked and no longer listened to God.

"And the Lord thy God will circumcise thy heart, and the heart of thy seed, to love the Lord thy God with all thy heart, and with all thy soul, that thou mayest live." (Deuteronomy 30:6)

"Circumcise yourselves to the Lord, and take away the foreskins of your heart, ye men of Judah and inhabitants of Jerusalem; lest my wrath go forth like fire, and burn so that none can quench it, because of the evil of your doings." (Jeremiah 4:4)

Unfortunately, the later priests were so out of touch with the deeper truths and inner sources of insight that they could not understand this.

Let's now compare the Mesoamerican Seven Ages with Edgar Cayce's Seven Stages. The correlation is curiously close, and makes sense when we are considered to be spiritual beings only temporarily incarnating in a material dimension of life.

Edgar Cayce, being the reincarnation of an ancient Egyptian high priest, brings imagery from ancient Egypt into his vision of the Ages or Stages.

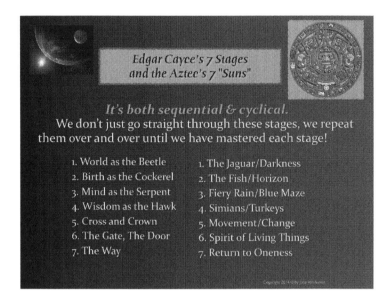

These are the 7 Ages, 7 Stages, 7 Cycles that the Children of God must experience in their soul growth. This was the plan developed by "the Elect" to ensure that the celestial Children of God could make their way through the difficult journey into self-centeredness and physicality, then back out into their original spirituality and heavenly oneness with their Creator and Infinite Eternal Life. The journey is sequential in the macrocosm but cyclical in microcosm of each soul's development. Each soul experiences and re-experiences each stage until it is fully perfected and master of each.

Here's Edgar Cayce's Q&A on the stages:

"Q: What were the symbols of the seven stages of man's development?

"A: The world as the beetle. Birth as the cockerel. The Mind as the serpent. Wisdom as the hawk. The varied activities in the cross, the crown, the gate, the door, the way." (281-25)

## The World as the Beetle

In Egyptian mysticism, the world is indeed seen as a beetle—a dung beetle! Yet the ancient Egyptians taught that from the dung of human life one can, as the dung beetle does, roll one's mess toward the rising Sun, plant a seed in it, and at high noon, when the Sun is at its highest, that seed will bring forth resurrection. In other words, out of the dung of life will come a new life, a new awareness.

## Birth as the Cockerel

The cockerel, or rooster, is the symbol for birth, the birth of our physical, lower selves. As the rooster, we were once cocksure of our beauty and virility, ready to fully incarnate in matter and to find mates. Yet the rooster, for all his physical lust, is irresistibly moved from deep within to crow when light penetrates the darkness as the Sun rises on a new day, a new opportunity.

The most famous cockerel in mystical lore is Abraxas, from the Egyptian Gnostics. The seven letters of his name were believed to be symbols of the seven rays of power – corresponding to the chakras. In the accompanying illustration of Abraxas we see imagery from Hinduism related to the kundalini and the reins for controlling the stallions of earthly senses and desires. This was an early age.

## Mind as the Serpent

Mind as the serpent is revealed in the Garden of Eden, when we listened to our mind's reasoning that we could disobey God and "not surely die," as God had warned. But, once eaten, the death was much worse than we had reasoned. Egyptian mysticism presents two serpents. One called Apep, who bites at the feet of our Ra-consciousness (God-consciousness), poisoning us with its distractions and temptations, as indicated in the biblical story of the Garden. The other is winged and lifts off the ground. It is a raised serpent that symbolizes our ability to raise our consciousness and energy sufficiently to know with higher awareness again.

## Wisdom as the Hawk

The hawk as wisdom is a symbol of our ability to see from higher perspectives, as the hawk does from a mile above the ground, floating on the winds of the spirit. This is the awakened higher mind. In ancient Egypt, the messiah was Horus, immaculately conceived by Isis; his icon is the hawk or falcon. The higher mind is our redeemer. It lifts us to a truer vision.

## The Cross and the Crown

The cross is symbolic of a key stage in our development. As Cayce stated in reading 2475-1 (and others), the crucifixion of our self-centered desires is required in order for us to awaken to our true, eternal nature and the real abilities of helpfulness that lie within our grasp as sons and daughters of God, as godlings in the image of God.

Cayce: "This is found to be experienced by all: that there was the necessity, for man's understanding, for the entering in of the Son of man, and that the Cross becomes the emblem of Him who offered himself, of himself. For that cause, for that purpose came He into the world, that He himself—in overcoming the world— might gain the Crown. So, each in their respective lives, their own experiences, find their cross overcoming the world, overcoming those things, those conditions, those experiences, that would not only enable them to meet the issues of life but to become heirs with Him of the Crown of Glory." (262-36) This age may correlate to the Piscean Age, that is rapidly coming to a close.

## The Gate, The Door

The gate or door is in our mind, heart, and body (as a chakra), and we control it with our free will. As the Spirit of God informed us through the disciple John in the Revelation: "As many as I love, I reprove and chasten; be zealous therefore, and repent. Behold, I stand at the door [of your heart, mind, and body] and knock; if any one hears my voice and opens the door, I will come in to him/her, and will sup with him/her, and he/she with me." (Revelation 3:19-20) Several Cayce readings indicate that the time we are entering is the time of opening the door to higher consciousness, greater love, and even higher chakras (there being 12 according to Cayce).

## The Way

The Way is expressed in the living of the two greatest commandments: 1. Love God with all our being, and 2. Love others as we would be loved. Love is the way. The essence of God is that vibration, that spirit we know as love. It is the single most powerful cleanser of all that hinders us—as Peter wrote: "Love covers a multitude of sins." (1 Peter 4:8) When we live lovingly, we know the glory that was ours before the world was, when we were conscious of being sons and daughters of God, when we were the morning stars.

# 3. Prophecies in the Bible

The Bible has many, many prophecies but we are only concerned with those that appear to speak to our times. With this in mind, I have chosen three major prophecy sections. The first is in the Book of Genesis, because it reveals who we really are, not who we now think we are. And that gives us an important insight into our destiny, and how that destiny is playing in our present times and future.

The second is Jesus' vision of the future as found in the Gospel of Matthew, Chapter 24. Jesus and his disciples were relaxing on the Mount of Olives next to the rebuilt Temple of Solomon. In answering a question about the magnificent temple Jesus gave a prophecy concerning the Temple and the future – a future that appears to speak to our times.

And the third prophecy is found in the last book of the Bible, The Revelation, also referred to as the Apocalypse by Roman Catholics. In this section we find the apostle John "in the Spirit on the Lord's Day" when he sees an elaborate 22-chapter vision of the future. John had been banished to the tiny Isle of Patmos in the Aegean Sea. While there he received the vision that is recorded and position as the last book of the Bible. It takes us from our Genesis to our ultimate destiny.

There are many more prophetic moments throughout the Bible that add to our study, and hopefully add to our understanding, but this book is focusing on those that most directly relate to our times.

Biblical prophecy has proved difficult to interpret. There are four reasons for this: 1. The strange imagery is an intentional effort to obscure meaning from those that are profane or simply curious. 2. The imagery in these prophecies comes from a deeper level of consciousness, thus requiring us to get into that level of consciousness before understanding comes. 3. Some of the messages are visionary, *holistic*, and often ethereal, yet we strive to interpret them linearly and literally according to mundane reality. 4. Some messages are dealing with the microcosm but we strive to interpret them in the macrocosm, not wanting to see how they actually relate to us as individuals. Despite this, the promise is: "Ask and it will be given to you; seek and you will find; knock and the door will be opened to you. For everyone who asks receives; he who seeks finds; and to him who knocks, the door will be opened." (Matthew 7:7-8)

We may also find that the biblical stories and prophecies are difficult to understand if one doesn't first realize that what we call "man" or humans were originally "gods" or spirits created in God's image and likeness, and at a deeper level we retain this even today. Here are statements from the Bible, Old and New Testament, that bear witness to this lost truth:

Genesis 1:27: *God created man [humanity] in his own image. In God's image he created them; male and female he created them.*

Psalm 82:6 – *I said, "You are gods; you are all sons (and daughters) of the Most High."*

John 10:34 – *Jesus answered them, "Is it not written in your Law, 'I have said you are gods'?"*

Acts 17:28-29 – *We are God's offspring.*

1 Corinthians 3:16 – *Do you not know that you are God's temple and that God's Spirit dwells in you?*

In many ancient cultures, such as India, Egypt, and Maya, the children of God were created and lived in the heavens, in the consciousness of God's presence, *before* they began to live in the flesh and the Earth. This is important to remember when trying to understand the predictions in the Scriptures.

## Our "Genesis" (*origin*)

There were *two* creations in Genesis. The first (Gen. 1:26-27) was when we were created in the image of God, which is *spirit* – "God is Spirit," John 4:23-24. Then, we were created again (Gen. 2:5-7) from the dust of the Earth – flesh. Now, there are two aspects to us, one spirit and godly, and the other flesh and human. Here are those passages from Genesis:

Gen. 1:26-27 – *So God created man in his own image, in the image of God he created them; male and female he created them.*

The Hebrew word for *God* in this verse is *Elohim*. Elohim is the infinite, omnipotent, omni-present Creator. The name *Elohim* is often shortened to *El* and used as part of a longer name. For example, *El Shaddai* means "God Almighty" (Genesis 49:24); *El Elyon* means "God Most High" (Deuteronomy 26:19); and *El Roi* means "God Who Sees" (Genesis 16:13). Personal names of people can include the name of God: Dani*el* ("El Is My Judge"), Nathana*el* ("Gift of El"), Samu*el* ("Heard by El"). Locations and groups can contain the shortened form of *Elohim*: Beth*el* ("House of El"), Jezre*el* ("El Will Sow"), and Mount Carm*el* ("God's Vineyard").

The second creation is recorded this way:

Gen. 2:4-8 – "This is the account of the heavens and the earth when they were created. When the Lord God made the earth and the heavens – and no shrub of the field had yet appeared on the earth and no plant of the field had yet sprung up, for the Lord God had not sent rain on the earth and there was no man to work the ground, but streams came up from the earth and watered the whole surface of the ground – the Lord God formed the man from the dust of the ground and breathed into his nostrils the breath of life, and the man became a living being. Now the Lord God had planted a garden in the east, in Eden; and there he put the man he had formed."

Notice after we were created in Genesis 1 in the image of Elohim (i.e., spirit, godly), there was still "no man (human) to work the ground." This was because we were not physical, not human, not in the flesh yet. As the last line indicates, God had not "formed" the man in matter yet – we were still godly spirits. In our deepest nature we are spirits, or as the ancient Egyptians called us, "godlings." Then, a different level of God, called the Lord God (Hebrew: *Yahweh Elohim*) created us a second time, now in the flesh – "from the dust of the earth."

Later in Genesis chapter 2, verses 18-25, the Lord God divides the androgynous being into *separate* male and female physical bodies. Remember the earlier statement: "male and female he created them," well these yin-yang genders were united in the original being prior to the separation. Why did God separate these? Here's the passage: "The Lord God said, It is not good for the man [human] to be by himself; I will make one like himself as a help to him." (Genesis 2:18) At this point in the creation story, we were still immortal beings that lived in direct contact with the Lord God in the Garden of Eden; or we think of this as a state of conscious awareness of God's presence – Paradise.

When we keep in mind that each being is both a godling and a human – or in biblical terms, a "son-daughter of God" and a "son-daughter of man" – then we can better understand why the biblical stories and prophecies are the way they are.

### The Curse

If one reads carefully, the *first* biblical prophecy is given by the Lord God to Adam and Eve as they leave the

Garden and the presence of the God. Because they freely ate of the fruit of the Tree of the Knowledge of Good and Evil, they now felt "naked" in God's all-knowing presence. They wanted to hide until they could again feel comfortable in the presence of God. This was not meant to be, but since they used their free-wills to make it so, they had to go out of the Presence. Of course, there was no way to go beyond the Infinite, the Whole, and the All-Knowing. But the Creator's love allowed an illusion of separation and privacy to exist.

In this next passage, the Lord God is speaking to our earthly selves. The Lord God does not want us to stay forever in the illusion of a separate reality, and so He has "cursed" reality in such a way that it will not give us ultimate satisfaction and contentment.

In the following passage, the serpent symbolizes the mind, but the part of our mind that is clever, seductive, and rationalizes or justifies going against what we know is not ideal.

Gen. 3:14-19 – "So the Lord God said to the serpent, 'Because you have done this, cursed are you above all the livestock and all the wild animals! You will crawl on your belly and you will eat dust all the days of your life.

"And I will put enmity between you and the woman, and between your offspring and her offspring; he [i.e., her offspring] will crush your head, and you will bruise his heel.'

"To the woman he said, 'I will greatly increase your pains in childbearing; with pain you will give birth to children. Your desire will be for your husband, and he will rule over you.'

"To Adam he said, 'Because you listened to your wife and ate from the tree which I commanded you, 'You must not eat of it,' cursed is the ground because of you; through painful toil you will eat of it all the days of your life. It will produce thorns and thistles for you, and you will eat the plants of the field. By the sweat of your brow you will eat your food until you return to the ground, since from it you were taken; for dust you are and to dust you will return.'"

Entry of the children of God into self-seeking, self-centered separation from God and the infinite creation was not part of the original plan. But since the children chose the flesh over the spirit, they were then cursed to struggle through the realms of flesh until they chose the spirit and the Garden of God's presence once again. And here is where we find a secret prophecy: The woman will produce an offspring that will crush the serpent's head, even as its evil bruises the savior's heel. This prophecy of special birth is important, and will appear throughout the biblical prophecies. In the meantime, life in the Earth will be hard for all concerned: serpent (selfish mind), woman the comforter and conceiver, and man the doer, tiller of the soil.

Gen. 3:21-24 – "The Lord God made garments of skin for Adam and Eve and clothed them. And the Lord God said, 'The man has now become like one of us, knowing good and evil. He must not be allowed to reach out his hand and take also from the Tree of Life and eat, and live forever.' So the Lord God banished him from the Garden of Eden to work the ground from which he had been taken.

"After he drove the man out, he placed on the east side of the Garden of Eden cherubim and a flaming sword flashing back and forth to guard the way to the Tree of Life."

Now we, the celestial, immortal children of God, have become predominantly terrestrial *and mortal*. We no longer have access to the Tree of Life. That is, not until we reach the end of this great journey described in the last book of the Bible, *The Revelation*. Here we find that the Tree of Life has been given back to us, and we may eat from it freely, and may drink the Water of Life freely. The story is from the loss of the Garden in Genesis to the "New Heaven" and "New Earth" of the final chapters in Revelation:

Rev. 21:1-6 – "Then I saw a new heaven and a new earth, for the first heaven and the first earth had passed away, and there was no longer any sea.

"I saw the Holy City, the new Jerusalem, coming down out of heaven from God, prepared as a bride beautifully dressed for her husband.

"And I heard a loud voice from the throne saying, 'Now the dwelling of God is with men [humanity], and he will live with them. They will be his people, and God himself will be with them and be their God.'

"He will wipe every tear from their eyes. There will be no more death or mourning or crying or pain, for the old order of things has passed away.

"He who was seated on the throne said, 'I am making everything new!' Then he said, 'Write this down, for these words are trustworthy and true.'

"He said to me: 'It is done. I am the Alpha and the Omega, the Beginning and the End. To him who is thirsty I will give to drink freely from the spring of the Water of Life.'"

Rev. 22:1-5 – "Then the angel showed me the River of the Water of Life, as clear as crystal, flowing from the throne of God and of the Lamb down the middle of the great street of the city.

"On each side of the river stood the Tree of Life, bearing twelve crops of fruit, yielding its fruit every month. And the leaves of the Tree are for the healing of the nations.

"No longer will there be any curse. The throne of God and of the Lamb will be in the city, and his servants will serve him.

"They will see his face, and his name will be on their foreheads.

"There will be no more night. They will not need the light of a lamp or the light of the sun, for the Lord God will give them light. And they will reign forever and ever." [Clearly if we don't need the Sun, then we are celestial spirits again!]

Rev. 2:7 – "He who has an ear, let him hear what the Spirit says.... To him who overcomes, I will give the right to eat from the Tree of Life, which is in the paradise of God."

As we can see in these verses, *it all ends happily ever after!*

Why is it so important to understand these elements of the Bible before we can understand the prophecies? Because the prophecies are all about the journey from the fall from Spirit and God's company, through the struggles with self-will and self-consciousness in the physical body and the Earth, then back into the full consciousness and oneness with the Spirit and God.

Now, when the Lord condemns or purges the flesh or the Earth, we understand that it is to *make room* for the spirit, which is the true nature of every being. When the prophecies scream for an end to Earth by fire, flood, plague, famine, and so on, we understand that it is a cry for the *rebirth of the spirit* by subduing the influences and demands of the flesh. Then, once the spirit is reborn, we unite these two aspects of ourselves in a "new heaven" and a "new earth." The curse is gone. All is new again. Every tear is wiped away, and our joy is full.

## Jesus' Prophecy on the Mount of Olives

Jesus left the temple and was walking away when his disciples came up to him to call his attention to its buildings. [This would have been about 33 A.D.]

"Do you see all these things?" he asked. "I tell you the truth, not one stone here will be left on another; everyone will be thrown down." [The temple was destroyed in 70 A.D.]

As Jesus was sitting on the Mount of Olives, the disciples came to him privately. "Tell us," they said, "when will this happen, and what will be the sign of your coming and of the end of the age?"

Our earthly selves naturally tend to understand time and prophecy from a *linear* perspective – first this will happen, then this and finally that. However, our higher selves and the spiritual realm see time and prophecy from a holistic perspective – this has, is, and will happen again and again until the rhythm, the pulse, the cycle is complete. Therefore, a great visionary can be speaking of a distant future as well as an imminent present. So, when Jesus answers what appears to us to be a question about the immediate future, he may actually be giving a more holistic answer. And later, when he says – "I tell you the truth, this generation will certainly not pass away until all these things have happened." – he may be correct, even though all these disciples died before the end times. Those listening to him will experience every bit of it within their microcosms, and ultimately within the macrocosm. Remember, all the dead will be called to life again. The Mount of Olives' teaching continues:

"Jesus answered: 'Watch out that no one deceives you.

"For many will come in my name, claiming, 'I am the Messiah,' and will deceive many.

"You will hear of wars and rumors of wars, but see to it that you are not alarmed. Such things must happen, but the end is still to come.

"Nation will rise against nation, and kingdom against kingdom. There will be famines and earthquakes in various places.

"All these are the beginning of birth pains.'"

See how Jesus uses this metaphor to explain the suffering and changes that must come about. The End Times are the birth of the Spirit. Like a woman in labor, we will suffer pain in our attempts to deliver our spiritual selves. The teaching continues:

"Then you will be handed over to be persecuted and put to death, and you will be hated by all nations because of me.

At that time many will turn away from the faith and will betray and hate each other, and many false prophets will appear and deceive many people."

In the 1900s we have seen the falling away from the faith. Who can forget the New York Times' headline: "God is dead!" And the false prophets have become so common that many deceived seekers have already been deprogrammed! But they keep coming. Some in the guise of religious leaders, some as political leaders, some as psychological liberators. Another amazing phenomenon has been the paganizing of the country that was founded with the slogan, "In God We Trust," printed on its money. The freedom this country provided the world has been used against it to undermine its values and purposes. Now, instead of a healthy separation of Church and State, we have a State that can have no semblance of trusting in or calling upon God.

The Mount of Olives' teaching continues: "Because of the increase of lawlessness, the love of most will grow cold, but he who stands firm to the end will be saved."

If there is one prophecy that I feel we all can

point to for evidence that we are in the latter days, it is this one. From Asia, through the U.S. and Europe and on into Russia, the Middle East, and India, lawlessness has taken a hold on daily life that has not been seen before. Crime is everywhere. Some countries are actually ruled by crime forces. Many fear that the newly-dissolved Soviet Union has left Russia a lawless country run by the forces of the underworld.

The Mount of Olives' teaching continues: "And this gospel of the kingdom will be preached in the whole world as a testimony to all nations, and then the end will come." Most Christians point to this prophecy as a sign that we are near to the end. The gospel of "love God with all thy being, and thy neighbor as thyself" has now been preached across the world. In the year 2000, Christianity was the religion of 31.2% of the world's population, the largest religion, with adherents in every country.

### The Abomination of Desolation

The prophecy continues:

"So, when you see standing in the holy place the abomination that causes desolation, spoken of through the prophet Daniel – let the reader understand – then let those who are in Judea flee to the mountains.

"Let no one on the roof of his house go down to take anything out of the house.

"Let no one in the field go back to get his cloak.

"How dreadful it will be in those days for pregnant women and nursing mothers!

"Pray that your flight will not take place in winter or on the Sabbath.

"For then there will be great distress, unequaled from the beginning of the world until now – and never to be equaled again.

"If those days had not been cut short, no one would survive, but for the sake of the elect those days will be shortened.

"At that time if anyone says to you, 'Look, here is the Messiah!' or, 'There he is!' do not believe it.

"For false Messiahs and false prophets will appear and perform great signs and miracles to deceive even the elect – if that were possible.

"See, I have told you ahead of time.

"So, if anyone tells you, 'There he is, out in the desert,' do not go out; or, 'Here he is, in the inner rooms,' do not believe it.

"For as lightning that comes from the east is visible even in the west, so will be the coming of the Son of Man.

"Wherever there is a carcass, there the vultures will gather.

"Immediately after the distress of those days the sun will be darkened, and the moon will not give its light; the stars will fall from the sky, and the heavenly bodies will be shaken.

"At that time the sign of the Son of Man will appear in the sky, and all the nations of the earth will mourn. They will see the Son of Man coming on the clouds of the sky, with power and great glory.

"And he will send his angels with a loud trumpet call, and they will gather his elect from the four winds, from one end of the heavens to the other.

"Now learn this lesson from the fig tree: As soon as its twigs get tender and its leaves come out, you know that summer is near.

"Even so, when you see all these things, you know that it is near, right at the door."

Jesus may be referring to the door of our consciousnesses, as well as the door into this world.

"I tell you the truth, this generation will certainly not pass away until all these things have happened.

"Heaven and earth will pass away, but my words

[logos] will never pass away."

Jesus is using the Greek word "logos" instead of "lalia" for "word." Logos means more than "word." It means the central essence of consciousness.

"No one knows about that day or hour, not even the angels in heaven, nor the Son, but only the Father.

"As it was in the days of Noah, so it will be at the coming of the Son of Man.

"For in the days before the flood, people were eating and drinking, marrying and giving in marriage, up to the day Noah entered the ark; and they understood nothing about what would happen until the flood came and took them all away. That is how it will be at the coming of the Son of Man."

There are several indications that Jesus is speaking about the inner and outer worlds and forces. The dire descriptions make it sound impossible to live through this coming birth: "There will be great distress, unequaled from the beginning of the world until now – and never to be equaled again." And, "If those days had not been cut short, no one would survive, but for the sake of the elect those days will be shortened." If you've ever watched a woman give birth, then you know how impossible it all seems. When asked how any can be saved, Jesus answered, "With man it is impossible, but with God all things are possible."

Individuals and the world may seem to be dying in a whirl of fire and flood, but the spark of the spirit within each soul will be delivered and reign forever and ever. We will not die, but all will be changed. With this in mind we can better grasp where the abomination of desolation should NOT be standing – it is within the hearts and minds of humanity, as individuals and as a soul group.

## A New Interpretation of The Revelation

Edgar Cayce's interpretation of the Revelation is very different than anything you've ever read. He explains: "The visions, the experiences, the names, the churches, the places, the dragons, the cities, all are but *emblems* of those forces that may war within the individual in its journey ... from the entering into the material manifestation to the entering into the glory, or the awakening in the spirit." (EC 281-16)

The seven churches in the Revelation symbolize the seven spiritual centers within our bodies – our chakras. A chakra is an energy generator inside our bodies and Cayce associates them with our endocrine glands, the glands that secrete powerful hormones. These are important to the spiritualization of our bodies. In the chapters about the spiritualization of our minds, the seven *awarenesses* correlate to seven lotuses, each having a mental point of view or perspective. The goal is to gain a higher view, a higher perspective. The chakras and the lotuses change as we raise our vibrations and our consciousness. In each case, the heavenly messenger begins by describing a characteristic of each spiritual center; it then acknowledges the center's strengths or virtues, followed by the center's shortcomings or vices. Finally, it gives the center a directive.

In breaking down the massive vision of the Revelation, Cayce explained that the first three chapters relate to spiritualizing the body, the next eight to spiritualizing the mind, the next nine to spiritualizing actions, and the final two chapters reveal the reward for completing the spiritual process.

There is no way for me to convey the whole interpretation of The Revelation in this section. But I will give the highlights. If you are interested in the whole interpretation, consider getting my book, *Edgar Cayce's Amazing Interpretation of the Revelation* (available from Amazon).

The seven churches of Asia Minor in the Revelation correlate to the seven endocrine glands which are the seven chakras:

Church–Gland–Chakra
1–Ephesus–Gonads–Root
2–Smyrna–Leydig Cells–Navel
3–Pergamos (Pergamum)–Adrenals–Solar Plexus
4–Thyatira–Thymus–Heart
5–Sardis–Thyroid–Throat
6–Philadelphia–Pineal–Crown
7–Laodicea–Pituitary–Third Eye

The Throne – 24 Elders – 7 Spirits
Lake of Glass – 4 Beasts

Now we see the throne of God and twenty-four elders, which Cayce identifies as the twelve paired (24) cranial nerves within our physical brains! Amazing how the imagery depicts physical anatomy – and how physical anatomy reflects spiritual channels and forces. The throne is before a "sea of glass like crystal," symbolizing the depths beneath outer consciousness and the stillness required to reach these levels of awareness.

Symbolically, energy is being emitted from the brain in the form of "flashes of lightning and sounds and peals of thunder." Seven "lamps of fire" are before the Throne, representing the "seven spirits of God," emblematic of our spiritual lotuses. These lotuses, or mental realms of consciousness, are awakening as this process continues. Their fragrance begins to subdue our earthly desires and lifts our body and mind to higher vibes and perceptions.

Also, around the throne are the "four beasts," seen also by Ezekiel and Daniel. Surprisingly, we find these same beasts represented in ancient Egyptian mysticism as the four children of Horus. Horus was the messiah in the ancient Egyptians, rescuing the world from Satan's domination. In one of the most famous scenes on ancient Egyptian papyruses, the four children of Horus are wrapped like mummies and standing on an open lotus. They are intoxicated by the fragrance of the holy flower, and are submissive before the throne of Osiris, a guardian of the way through the Netherworld to the Heavens. This scene reflects how the four lower chakras become intoxicated by the heavenly fragrance of the opening lotuses and turn their attention to the spiritual.

According to Cayce, these four beasts are "the four destructive influences that make the greater desire for the carnal forces, that arise as the beasts within self to destroy." (EC 281-16) We have learned what these destructive influences are from the heavenly messenger's comments to the first four churches, or spiritual centers: (1) leaving our first love; (2) fear; (3) anger, impulsive reactions, and spirit-killing urges; and (4) living life without love and ideals.

All of these destructive influences were personified in Cain. In Hebrew Abel means "breath," symbolizing our spiritual self, while Cain means "acquired," symbolizing our growing ego and self-centered state. Though Cain at first sought God's love, he later did not desire it. He killed his brother impulsively in anger and spitefulness, only to then become so afraid that he could not go on without God's promise of protection. Finally, he goes out to live life for himself and his own gratification, without any spiritual interests or intentions. In the book of Job, Satan claimed that Job was the same as Cain, having no interest in God and the spiritual life, and would curse God to His face if He touched Job's physical life and body. Cayce said that these destructive influences must be dealt with and subdued (EC 281-16); as God said to Cain, "Sin is crouching at the door [of your consciousness], its desire is for you, but *you must master it.*" (Genesis 4:7)

## The Cleansings

Now, with the seven spiritual centers awakened, the higher self and the life force rising, the lower urges subdued, and our spiritual-self seated again on the Throne, we begin a series of cleansings. This begins with John's vision of the famous "Four Horsemen of the Apocalypse," who ride out with specific colors, implements, and missions.

We are a microcosm of our Infinite Eternal Creator, thus all that is in the macrocosm has a reflexive presence *within* us. (EC 2984-1) At first glance, it may seem paradoxical that these outer influences are also within us and that cosmic things find a relating point within our being, but as the Ancient Egyptian god Hermes (Thoth) stated: "As within so without, as above so below." The body and the mind are arranged in a manner that reflects the arrangement of the universe.

When the cleansings are completed, loud voices from heaven cry out, "The kingdom of the world has become the kingdom of the Lord, and of His Messiah; and He will reign forever and ever." The twenty-four elders worship God, saying, "We give Thee thanks, O Lord God, the Almighty, who is and was, because Thou has taken Thy great power and has begun to reign." Then all cells of the body are judged according to their level of oneness and atonement with this new reign. And then, the temple of God is opened, and the Ark of the Covenant appears in the temple, causing flashes of lightning, peals of thunder, earthquakes, and a great hailstorm. The physical body has now reached a level of cleansing, vibration, and oneness to become the temple of God. Cayce describes it this way:

"As the Book of Life then is opened, there is seen the effect of that which now has been attained by the opening of the system, the body, the mind; all of those effects that have been created by the ability of the entity to attune self to the consciousness of being at-one with the Divine within. Now we see those in the material world using these influences for self-exaltation, self-indulgence, and self-glorification; and yet we see those using same for the glory, the understanding, the knowledge, and the wisdom of the Father." (EC 281-33)

There is now a curious passage in chapter 20 that speaks of two resurrections and two deaths, the first and the second. Cayce explains it this way:

The first [resurrection] is of those who have not tasted death in the sense of the dread of same. The second [resurrection] is of those who have gained the understanding that in Him there is no death."

EC 281-37

Here Cayce distinguishes between two groups of people: those who have lost their fear of death because they believe and have faith in the promise of an afterlife, and those whose transition with the Lord is akin to falling asleep to this world and awakening within the heavens. These two groups are also distinguished in the Revelation when the angel instructs, "He who is righteous, let him do righteousness still. He who is holy, let him be holy still." (Rev 22:11) The difference is that the holy ones have the presence of God awakened within the temple of their bodies and minds, while the righteous do good for goodness' sake. The true Kabbalist seeks to fully experience God's presence and contain this holiness in the orbs of his or her being – not simply to believe in God but to know God.

# 4. The Prophecies of Edgar Cayce

In the mid 1920s to 1944, Edgar Cayce produced more material on the End Times and Earth Changes than any other source I know of. The volume of material is staggering. But what is more important is that much of the material is very specific to what will happen and when.

Edgar Cayce (pronounced, KAY-see) was born on a farm near Hopkinsville, Kentucky, on March 18, 1877. As a child, he displayed unusual powers of perception. At the age of six he told his parents that he could see and talk with "visions," sometimes of relatives who had recently died, and even angels. He could also sleep with his head on his schoolbooks and wake with a photographic recall of their contents; even sighting the page upon which the answer appeared.

The routine he used for conducting a trance-like "reading" was to recline on a couch, hands folded across his forehead, then upon seeing a white light, he would place his hand over his solar-plexus, and begin breathing deeply. Eventually, his eyelids would begin fluttering (RIM, rapid-eye-movement that precedes sleep and dreams) and his breathing would become deep and rhythmical. This was the signal to the conductor (usually his wife) to make verbal contact with Cayce's subconscious by giving a suggestion. Unless this procedure was timed to synchronize with his fluttering eyelids and the change in his breathing, Cayce would proceed beyond his trance state and simply fall fast asleep. However, once the suggestion was made, the light moved and Cayce would "move" with it, mentally of course. He could then describe the client as though he or she were sitting right next to him, his mind functioning much as an x-ray scanner, seeing into every organ of their body, and the history of their body's experiences. When he was finished, he would say, "Ready for questions." However, in many cases his mind would have already anticipated the patient's questions, answering them during the main session. Eventually, he would say, "We are through for the present," whereupon the conductor would give the suggestion to return to normal consciousness.

If this procedure were in any way violated, Cayce would be in serious personal danger. On one occasion, he remained in a trance state for three days and had actually been given up for dead by the attending doctors.

At each session, a stenographer (usually his personal secretary) would record everything Cayce said. Sometimes, during a trance session, Cayce would even correct the stenographer's spelling. It was as though his mind were in touch with everything around him and beyond.

Each client was identified with a number to keep their names private. For example, hypnotic material for Edgar Cayce is filed under the number 294. His first "reading," as they were called, would be numbered 294-1, and each subsequent "reading" would increase the dash number (294-2, 294-3, and so on). Some numbers refer to groups of people, such as the Study Group, 262; and some numbers refer to specific research or guidance readings, such as the 254 series, containing the Work readings dealing with the overall work of the organization that grew up around him, and the 364 and 996 series containing the readings on Atlantis.

His discourses were nicknamed "readings" because he felt that he was reading the person, or their Book of Life; and on broader questions the Akashic Record that records all the activities of the Creation!

It was August 10, 1923 before anyone thought to

ask the "sleeping" Cayce for insights beyond physical health – questions about life, death and human destiny. In a small hotel room in Dayton, Ohio, Arthur Lammers asked the first set of philosophical questions that were to lead to an entirely new way of using Cayce's strange abilities. It was during this line of questioning that Cayce first began to talk about reincarnation as though it were as real and natural as the functions of a physical body. This shocked and challenged Cayce and his family. They were deeply religious people, doing this work to help others because that's what their Christian faith taught. Reincarnation was not part of their reality. Yet, the healings and help continued to come. So, the Cayce family continued with the physical material, but cautiously reflected on the strange philosophical material. Ultimately, the Cayces began to accept the ideas, though not as "reincarnation" per se. Edgar Cayce preferred to call it, "The Continuity of Life." As a child, he began to read the Bible from front to back, and did so for every year of his life. He felt that it did contain much evidence that life, the true life in the Spirit, is continual. Physical birth and death were not the beginning and end of a person's spiritual life.

Eventually, Edgar Cayce, following advice from his own readings, moved to Virginia Beach, Virginia, and set up a hospital where he continued to conduct his "Physical Readings" for the health of others. But he also continued this new line of readings called "Life Readings." From 1925 through 1944, he conducted some 2500 of these Life Readings, describing the past lives of individuals as casually as if everyone understood reincarnation were a reality. Such subjects as deep-seated fears, mental blocks, vocational talents, innate urges and abilities, marriage difficulties, child training, etc., were examined in the light of what the readings called the "karmic patterns" resulting from previous lives spent by the individual's soul on the Earth plane.

When he died on January 3, 1945, in Virginia Beach, he left well over 14,000 documented stenographic records of the telepathic-clairvoyant readings he had given for more than 6,000 different people over a period of forty-three years.

The readings constitute one of the largest and most impressive records of psychic perception. Together with their relevant records, correspondence and reports, they have been cross-indexed under thousands of subject headings and placed at the disposal of doctors, psychologists, students, writers and investigators who still come to examine them. Of course, they are also available to the general public in topical books or in complete volumes of the readings, as well as digitally online, and on CD-ROM for PCs and Macs.

A foundation known as the Association for Research and Enlightenment (A.R.E.) was founded in 1932 to preserve these readings. As an open-membership research society, it continues to index and catalog the information, initiate investigation and experiments, and conduct conferences, seminars and lectures. The A.R.E. also has one of largest libraries of parapsychological and metaphysical books in the world, second only to the Vatican Library.

### Problem Interpreting the Cayce Visions

Edgar Cayce's readings do present some difficulties in interpretation and understanding. First, they are somewhat difficult to read, mostly due to their syntax and the presence of archaic or biblical terms and style. They are *written* records of a *verbal* presentation, a process that occasionally does not carry the full intent that was expressed, and punctuation can significantly change the meaning or intent of the voiced statement. Also, most of the readings were given to *specific* people with uniquely *personal* perspectives and prejudices on the topics being discussed, and therefore, the responses were slanted to fit the seeker's perspective. For example, in a reading for one person, Cayce recommends one marriage for life, to another he recommends never getting married, and to a third he encourages him to marry at least twice before he'd become a good husband. In the few cases where a reading was purposefully for broader presentation to many people, even the masses, the "sleeping" Cayce was still somewhat at the mercy and wisdom of the those directing the session and asking the questions. Cayce and his wife Gertrude, and their assistant Gladys, were very conscientious people, always seeking to be exact and true to the original intent of the reading. As I indicated earlier, the "sleeping" Cayce would occasionally stop his direct discourse to give an aside to Gladys about the way she was recording the material, correcting spelling, or giving a clarifying explanation of something he had just said.

Finally, because some of Cayce's readings cover so many points or issues within the text, it can be difficult to determine which one he is referring to when the paragraphs are so complex. Despite all of this, with practice, one can become familiar enough with the syntax, terms and "thys," "thees," and "thous"; a repetitive use of the word "that"; and the complex thought pattern, that one can learn to read and understand the Cayce readings fairly easily. Still, experienced readers of Cayce's work can read the same readings and come up with differing views as to what they mean.

For example, on this topic of End Times and Earth Changes, there are differing views within the A.R.E. as to just what is going to happen, if anything. Some believe that the Cayce readings have predicted Earth changes that simply have not occurred; in other words, he was wrong, and could therefore be wrong about everything. Others say that these readings were misinterpreted, and the changes spoken of are yet to come. Some believe that there are Cayce readings that say the Earth changes are all subject to modification or even suspension of their prophesied outcome if humanity makes some changes in their hearts and minds. Others believe Cayce's readings state that some Earth changes are virtual actualities waiting for their time to manifest; they are simply preordained destiny. The sheer volume and complexity of the material makes it difficult for everyone to agree on what is in the readings and what they mean. I hope I can clarify some of this for all our sakes.

Most of the Cayce readings presented in this book are edited for clarity, readability and focus on the point at hand. However, I've included all the reading numbers so you can review the originals.

### Edgar Cayce Prophecies

During the Great Depression, Cayce lost his magnificent building on the hill overlooking the ocean in Virginia Beach, Virginia. It depressed him so much, that some were concerned about the quality of his readings during this time. This is particularly true of the Earth-change readings given through the sleeping Cayce that included an entity called "Halaliel." I have deliberately kept these readings separate. In this way I can show how Cayce continued to give similar Earth-change readings long after Halaliel was gone. Nevertheless, the Halaliel readings have some of the most interesting perspectives on these prophecies of change. Therefore, let's begin with them.

### Prophecies Conveyed Through Cayce by Halaliel

Halaliel (pronounced *Hala-lee-EL*) first identified himself through the sleeping Cayce on October 15, 1933 during a Study Group reading on the lesson titled, "Day and

Night." There had been 55 readings given to this Study Group. Occasionally, messages had come through the sleeping Cayce from other entities in the spirit realms, but never was the complete reading credited to a single spirit entity. The reading began and continued as usual, but it ended on a strange note. Here is the last question of this reading and the answer given.

262-56: "Q: Comment upon the following. Does it carry any light of truth?

"The Creator, in seeking to create a being worthy of companionship, realized that such a being would result only from having free will and exercising its divine inheritance through its own efforts to find its Maker. Thus, making the choice really a Divine one has caused the existence of states of consciousness, that would indeed tax the free will of a soul; thus light and darkness. Truly, only those tried "so as by fire" can enter in.

"A: The only variation that we would make is that all souls in the beginning were *one* with the Father. The separation, or turning away, brought evil. Then there became the necessity of the awareness of self's being out of accord with blessedness, or out of the realm of blessedness; and, as given of the Son, "yet learned he obedience through the things which he suffered."

"COME, my children! Ye no doubt have gained from the comment this day, a new initiate has spoken in or through this channel; Halaliel, that was with those in the beginning who warred with those that separated themselves and became as naught.".

The closing line is referring to the legendary battle between the angels of rebellion, led by Lucifer, and the angels of light, led by Michael. Apparently, Halaliel was among those angels of light that warred with the separating angels, who later became known as the Fallen Angels or Dark Angels.

The next time Halaliel is mentioned by the sleeping Cayce is on October 24, 1933 at the morning reading. This time the reading is a "research reading" dealing with the subjects of psychic phenomena, spiritism and spiritualism. The reading ends very strangely again, giving a list of entities who can be of help in gaining a better understanding of these concepts, instructing the conductor (Gertrude Cayce, Edgar's wife) to call these "forces" to be present for the next reading.

5756-10: "The forces gathered here may be used in gaining this concept. As ye seek, ask first if all these are present: Lamech, Confucius, Tamah, Halaliel, Hebe, Ra, Ra-Ta, John.

That very afternoon, at the 3:00 p.m. reading, Gertrude began the reading in accord with the morning suggestion.

5756-11: "GC (Gertrude Cayce): If the forces Lamech, Confucius, Tamah, Halaliel, Hebe, Ra, Ra-Ta, John are present, we seek the answer to the following question."

Gladys' notes at the end of this reading include this statement: "Edgar Cayce said on waking that he would like to always feel surrounded by as helpful influences as he did this time."

On January 7, 1934 the 57th Study Group reading was given and one of those in attendance asked, "Who is Halaliel?" Here's the answer:

262-57: "One in and with whose courts Ariel fought when there was the rebellion in heaven. Now, where is heaven? Where is Ariel, and who was he? A companion of Lucifer or Satan, and one that made for the disputing of the influences in the experiences of Adam in the Garden."

Clearly, we are dealing with the legendary war of the angels. All the angels were originally created in the image of the Creator, but through the misuse of free will, some rebelled against the cooperative spirit of Oneness. This rebellion would not be allowed; it was like a cancer in the Universal Consciousness. So, they were driven from heaven until such time that they repented of their self-seeking ways and re-tuned themselves to the Creator's harmonious spirit of oneness. Notice that the literal meanings of their names are quite beautiful and powerful, as they were originally intended to be: Ariel means "lion of God" and Lucifer means "light giver." The name Satan is actually from a Hebrew word that simply means "adversary." This is why the Messiah is often called the "advocate;" he is our counter influence to the adversary.

At the end of this reading, Gladys noted that Edgar Cayce had a slightly different experience during the reading. Normally, he would go to the Hall of Records to receive the Book of Life (the records) of the individual for whom the reading was being given. This time he felt that a "group activity" took place in the back of the Hall of Records where he received the records. Could this have been the group of Lamech, Confucius, Tamah, Halaliel, Hebe, Ra, Ra-Ta, and John?

The very next time Halaliel is mentioned is on the 8th of January, 1934, in a reading for a female society leader and Theosophist, #443. She had been asking a series of very involved questions about mysticism and spiritual truth, then she asked:

443-3: "Q: How high is the source that this information is being given from?

"A: From the universal forces, and as emanated through the teacher that gives same - as one that has been given – Halaliel.

A few days later, on the 19th, we get the first earth changes material delivered by Halaliel, or at least some portion of the reading was from Halaliel because he says so in the midst of the reading. This whole reading is unusual. For the first time they are using a recording instrument to record the reading. Instead of Gertrude conducting, their eldest son, Hugh Lynn Cayce was the conductor, and in his opening suggestion to Edgar, he instructs Edgar to stop every fifteen minutes so the recording device can be reloaded. Amazingly, the entranced Edgar stops exactly every fifteen minutes throughout the reading, even if he is in mid-sentence. Here is Hugh Lynn's opening suggestion and the sleeping Edgar's response:

3976-15: "HLC: We seek at this time such information as will be of value and interest to those present regarding the spiritual, mental and physical changes which are coming to the earth. You will tell us what part we may play in meeting and helping others to understand these changes. At the end of each fifteen-minute period you will pause, until I tell you to continue, while the recording instrument is being arranged. You will speak distinctly at a normal rate of speech, and you will answer the questions which we ask.

"EC: Yes; as each of you gathered here have your own individual development, yet as each seeks to be a channel of blessings to the fellow man, each attunes self to the Throne of universal information. And, there may be accorded you that which may be beneficial, not only in thine own experience, but that which will prove helpful, hopeful, in the experience of others."

From here, the reading goes into a brief description of the number and nature of the spirit entities that are gathered about them now to help with this reading. Then, the reading tells of the return of one of their members to the earth to help with this coming period of earth changes. The returning entity is the disciple John the Beloved. Then the reading begins to address the coming earth changes. Remember, the reading is being given in January of 1934.

3976-15: "As to the material changes that are to be as an omen, as a sign to those that this is shortly to come to pass - as has been given of old, the sun will be darkened and the earth shall be broken up in diverse places - and THEN shall be PROCLAIMED - through the spiritual interception in the hearts and minds and souls of those that have sought His way - that HIS star has appeared, and will point the way for *those that enter into the holy of holies* in themselves. For, God the Father, God the Teacher, God the director, in the minds and hearts of men, must ever be IN those that come to know Him as first and foremost in the seeking of those souls; for He is first the GOD to the individual and as He is exemplified, as He is manifested in the heart and in the acts of the body of the individual, then He becomes manifested before men. And those that seek in the latter portion of the year of our Lord (as ye have counted in and among men) '36, He will appear."

My italics isolate the phrase that fits so well with the prophet Daniel's visions. Recall that one of Daniel's visions was entering the sanctuary, the holy of holies *within* each of us. Here Halaliel speaks to the same activity, saying that those who do go within their sanctuary will know, will be guided. The "He will appear" phrase is developed further elsewhere in the Cayce readings. Cayce says that the Messiah first comes in the hearts and minds of those that seek this influence; then it moves into the physical realm, ultimately becoming fully manifest, as we are, incarnate. Cayce says, "He will walk and talk with people of every clime." Here, Halaliel is stating that the beginning of this process is in 1936, for those that seek within themselves. Then, Halaliel continues, focusing on earth changes:

"As to the changes physical again: The earth will

be broken up in the western portion of America. The greater portion of Japan must go into the sea. The upper portion of Europe will be changed as in the twinkling of an eye. Land will appear off the east coast of America. There will be the upheavals in the Arctic and in the Antarctic that will make for the eruption of volcanoes in the Torrid areas [areas between the Tropic of Cancer and the Tropic of Capricorn divided by the equator], and there will be shifting then of the poles - so that where there has been those of a frigid or the semi-tropical will become the more tropical, and moss and fern will grow. And these will *begin* in those periods in '58 to '98, when these will be proclaimed as the periods when His light will be seen again in the clouds. As to times, as to seasons, as to places, ALONE is it given to those who have named the name - and who bear the mark of those of His calling and His election in their bodies. To them it shall be given.

"As to those things that deal with the mental of the earth, these shall call upon the mountains to cover many. As ye have seen those in lowly places raised to those of power in the political, in the machinery of nations' activities, so shall ye see those in high places reduced and calling on the waters of darkness to cover them. And those that in the inmost recesses of theirselves awaken to the spiritual truths that are to be given, and those places that have acted in the capacity of teachers among men, the rottenness of those that have ministered in places will be brought to light, and turmoils and strifes shall enter. And, as there is the wavering of those that would enter as emissaries, as teachers, from the throne of life, the throne of light, the throne of immortality, and wage war in the air with those of darkness, then know ye the Armageddon is at hand. For with the great numbers of the gathering of the hosts of those that have hindered and would make stumbling blocks for man and his weaknesses, they shall wage war with the spirits of light that come into the earth for this awakening; that have been and are being called by those of the sons of men into the service of the living God. For He, as ye have been told, is not the God of the dead, not the God of those that have forsaken Him, but those that love His coming, that love His associations among men - the God of the LIVING, the God of Life! For, He IS Life."

At this point, the reading shifts back to the return of apostle John the Beloved, whose name is stated as "John Peniel" (pronounced, pen-ee-EL but often said *pen-eel*). Of course, "peniel" means "face of God" in Hebrew, and was the name Jacob gave to the place where he met God face-to-face and his own name was changed to *Israel*, which means "strives with God." The reading says that John will be known in America by those that have gone through the regeneration in their bodies, minds and spirits, and that he will give "the new order of things." John will be able to make these things "PLAIN in the minds of men, that they may know the truth, the life, the light, will make them free." Then, the reading goes into an intense, inspiring call to awaken, filled with biblical phrases and ending with Halaliel identifying himself as the deliverer of this information:

3976-15: "I have declared this, that has been delivered unto me to give unto you, ye that sit here and that hear and that see a light breaking in the east, and have heard, have seen thine weaknesses and thine fault-findings, and know that He will make thy paths straight if ye will but live that YE KNOW this day. Then, may the next step, the next word, be declared unto thee. For ye in your weakness have known the way, through that as ye have made manifest of the SPIRIT of truth and light that has been proclaimed into this earth, that has been committed unto the keeping of Him that made of

Himself no estate but who brought into being all that ye see manifest in the earth. He has declared this message unto thee: "Love the Lord thy God with all thine heart," and the second is like unto it, "Love thy neighbor as thyself." Who is thine neighbor? Him that ye may aid in whatsoever way that he, thy neighbor, thy brother, has been troubled. Help him to stand on his own feet. For such may only know the acceptable way. The weakling, the unsteady, must enter into the crucible and become as naught, even as He, that they may know the way. I, Halaliel, have spoken."

This is followed by a series of questions from the participants. The first question deals directly with the earth changes, and it is here that Halaliel begins to get into trouble with future students of this material. They point out that the first question asked what earth changes would occur "this year;" that would have been 1934. But the answer clearly does not address 1934, nor did any of the changes mentioned occur in '34. Perhaps Halaliel's consciousness was too vast to focus on '34, or '34 never made a sufficient impact on his consciousness to get a specific answer. So Halaliel keeps on discussing the earth changes as a whole, over many years to come. Perhaps the initial suggestion to give information about any earth changes was still the dominant suggestion, and Hugh Lynn did not sufficiently emphasize that he now only wanted changes that would physically occur in 1934. Whatever the reason, it is clear that Halaliel did not focus on 1934:

3976-15: "Q: What are the world changes to come this year physically?

"A: The earth will be broken up in many places. The early portion will see a change in the physical aspect of the west coast of America. There will be open waters in the northern portions of Greenland. There will be new lands seen off the Caribbean Sea, and DRY land will appear. There will be the falling away in India of much of the material suffering that has been brought on a troubled people. There will be the reduction of one risen to power in central Europe to naught. The young king son will soon reign [in Germany]. In America in the political forces we see a re-stabilization of the powers of the peoples in their own hands, a breaking up of the rings, the cliques in many places. South America shall be shaken from the uppermost portion to the end, and in the Antarctic off of Tierra Del Fuego LAND, and a strait with rushing waters."

Earlier in this reading you'll notice that the earth changes are to "*begin* in those periods '58 – '98." I believe that Halaliel's consciousness was still filled with this information, and continued to reveal to us the overall sequence of the changes. Now Hugh Lynn shifts the topic to political issues dealing with 1934 in Germany and America with a series of questions. Then, he ends with an open question for any more advice, and we get this:

3976-15: "Q: Is there any further counsel or advice for us gathered here, which will enable us to understand better our responsibility?

"A: All gathered here in the name of God who is the Father, to those that seek to know His ways - and who is as something outside the veil of their understanding *unless sought!* The counsel of the Father, of that God-Mother comes in each soul that seeks to know the biddings; not as one that would reap vengeance but rather as the loving, MERCIFUL Father. For, as ye show mercy, so may the Father show mercy to thee. As ye show the wisdom, as ye show the love of thy fellow man, so may the love be shown, so may the wisdom, so may the guiding steps day-by-day be shown thee. Be ye joyous in the Lord, knowing that He is ever present with those that seek His face. He is not in heaven, but makes heaven in thine own heart, if ye accept Him. He, God, the Father, is present and manifest in that ye mete to your fellow man in thine own experience.

"Would ye know the Father, be the father to thy brother. Would ye know the love of the Father, SHOW thy love to thy faltering, to thy erring brother - but to those that seek, not those that condemn."

I simply cannot throw this material out because Halaliel did not correctly address the 1934 physical earth changes question! There is simply too much in this reading that is obviously from a very high source of attunement and guidance. I do not see Halaliel exalting himself or attempting to attract attention to himself. He seems to be directing everyone's attention to God – God within themselves; exactly what Jesus encouraged. The false prophets Jesus warned us about were those that would say the Messiah is "over here or there," rather than within us. Halaliel is saying exactly what Jesus taught, "the kingdom of heaven is within you." These earth-change prophecies should not be ignored because Cayce missed the focusing question about "this year."

Halaliel continues to make appearances in the readings over the next several months of 1934. On the 9th of September, the Study Group met again for its 71st reading, receiving what they believed to be further information about Halaliel, though it is not clearly stated as such in the reading. Here's what they heard and assumed to be referring to Halaliel [note: Gladys told me that when Cayce raised his voice, she all-capped the words, as you see in the beginning of this readings].

262-71: "TO ALL WE WOULD GIVE: Be patient. That part thou hast chosen in such a work is born of truth. Let it come in and be a part of thy daily life. Look in upon the experiences, for, as will be seen, my children, *there has been appointed one that may aid thee in thy future lessons, and he will be thy teacher, thy guide, one sent through the power of thine own desires.* Thine own selves, then, may present his being, meeting, living, dwelling, with thee. *Not the Christ, but His messenger, with the Christ from the beginning, and is to other worlds what the Christ is to this earth.*" [my italics]

Some in the Study Group, including Hugh Lynn Cayce, wanted to reject Halaliel's help, fearful that they might be led away from Christ. These were hard times, and there was much anxiety about the dark forces behind these hard times. They ultimately did reject his help and asked that only the Christ guide them. Gladys notes that "two or three in the group were still not convinced that we were right in rejecting Halaliel's help in preparing the lessons." Whatever the truth about Halaliel, we hear nothing from him again, and his earth-changes comments are often questioned by those that feel he was not a high source, despite the reading's comments to the contrary. Fortunately, we have many other Cayce readings on earth changes that support and enhance Halaliel's prophecies.

### Prophecies without Halaliel

After the Great Depression, around 1936, Cayce began to get over the loss of his center, and many felt that he was in a good place to give his best readings. This first reading occurs on January 20, 1936, two years after the Halaliel readings ended. As you can see, Cayce is still conveying a version of major changes for our world. Basically, it is a personal reading for Mr. 270, dealing with many personal issues, but toward the end of the reading, 270 asks the following question:

270-35: "Q: What is the primary cause of earthquakes? Will San Francisco suffer from such a catastrophe this year [1936]? If so, give date, time and information for the guidance of this body, who has personal property, records and a wife, all of which it wishes safety.

"A: We do not find that this particular district (San Francisco) in the present year ['36] will suffer the great MATERIAL damages that HAVE been experienced heretofore. While portions of the country will be affected, we find these will be farther EAST than San Francisco - or those SOUTH, where there has NOT been heretofore the greater activity."

"If there are the greater activities in the Vesuvius, or Pelée, then the southern coast of California - and the areas between Salt Lake and the southern portions of Nevada - may expect, within the three months following the greater activity, an inundation by the earthquakes. But these, as we find, are to be more in the southern than in the northern hemisphere."

This fits very well with Halaliel's prophecy, "The earth will be broken up in the western portion of America."

Obviously, the Cayce readings predicted significant changes for America; the most drastic changes will be in South America, but North America will have its share. The changes to the western coast of North America are apparently triggered by two volcanoes, Vesuvius in Italy and Pelée on the island of Martinique in the West Indies.

In 1941, Cayce gave another detailed description of the prophesied earth changes.

1152-11: "As to conditions in the geography of the world, of the country, changes are gradually coming about.

"In the next few years lands will appear in the Atlantic as well as in the Pacific. And what is the coastline of many a land now will be the bed of the ocean. Even many of the battlefields of the present [1941 WW II] will be ocean, will be the seas, the bays, the lands over which the *new* order will carry on their trade.

"Portions of the now east coast of New York, or New York City itself, will disappear. This will be another generation though. The southern portions of Carolina, Georgia will disappear [Could he be referring to movement along the major fault in Charlestown, SC?]. This will come first.

"The waters of the lakes [Great Lakes] will empty into the Gulf [of Mexico] rather than the waterway over which such discussions have been recently made [St. Lawrence Seaway]. It would be well if the new waterway were prepared.

"Then the area where the entity is now located [Virginia Beach] will be among the safety lands, as will be what is now Ohio, Indiana, and Illinois and much of the southern portion of Canada and the eastern portion of Canada. While, the western land is to be disturbed."

Ms. 1152 finishes this reading with some very direct questions about New York City, Los Angeles and San Francisco.

1152-11: "Q: I have for many months felt that I should move away from New York City.

"A: This is well. There is too much unrest. There will continue to be the character of vibrations that to this body will be disturbing. Eventually, there will be the destructive forces there - though these will be in the next generation.

"Q: Will Los Angeles be safe?

"A: Los Angeles, San Francisco, most all of these will be among those that will be destroyed before New York even."

In 1942, a person asked if their business location would be safe until their lease expired. The answer was that those locations on the mainland would be safe, but not those on Manhattan Island [412-13]. The trouble with this reading is that the lease in question was for only one year, expiring in 1943, and Manhattan Island is still there. Is this another example of a vision of the future affecting Cayce's deeper consciousness so profoundly that it cannot relate to the one-year time frame of the question? Or, is it simply a mistake?

## The Supply and Demand for Food

The previous few readings may give a sense of specific changes in the physical structure to portions of North America, but the next few readings indicate that the extreme hardships prophesied will actually come to the country as a whole. For example, in 1942, Mr. 416 asks if he should hold onto his lots and acreage in Virginia Beach or sell. The sleeping Cayce tells him to sell the lots and hold onto the acreage because it will be needed to grow food for himself and those closely associated with him during "the extreme periods through which all portions of the country must pass." [416-17] Since this warning is certainly *after* the Great Depression, we can assume that another cycle of difficulty with the material necessities of life is coming. As of yet, we have seen no evidence of any problems with food excepting specific locations where hurricanes, earthquakes, fires, and floods have destroyed the network of modern services. In reading 257-254, given in 1943, Cayce responds to a question about the expected changes in America with this answer: "These conditions have not changed. The hardships with the supply and demand for foods in this country have not begun yet." In 1944, in reading 3620-1, he says "Anyone who can buy a farm is fortunate and buy it if you don't want to grow hungry in some days to come."

## The Great Pole Shift

In the Halaliel reading that dealt so clearly and specifically with coming Earth changes, a reference was made to a shifting of the Earth poles. Halaliel said that the changes would begin during the period between

1958 and 1998, but he did not say exactly when the pole shift would occur. In a life reading for Mr. 826 in 1936, Cayce gives a more exact dating. Still, the implication in both Halaliel readings in '34 and this one in '36 is that the pole shift is a developing event over a period of some years, beginning in the '58-'98 range and culminating in the actual shifting in 2000 to 2001, or very near these dates.

When asked "What great change or the beginning of what change, if any, is to take place in the Earth in the year 2000 to 2001 A.D.?" Cayce answered: "When there is the shifting of the poles; or a new cycle begins." The Maya also saw a new era beginning in the first years of the new millennium but, according to their artifacts, it begins when the present age of "Movement" ends on December 21-23, 2012 AD. However, there may be no conflict between Cayce and the Maya, because pole shifts take a long time to complete the change. The north and south poles of the axis around which our planet spins are wobbling. Astronomers believe the wobble has been occurring for ages and causes the North Pole to point to different Pole Stars or North Stars in these present times. How often this occurs is unclear. According to leading scientific teams at major research centers, axis shifts have only occurred every few million or billion years and taken millions of years to be completed. According to other worthy sources (e.g., Encyclopedia Britannica Educational Corporation, York Films, and *The Learning Channel*), the wobble changes the Pole Star about every 24,000 to 26,000 years. In Hinduism a full day and night in the Brahma equals 24,000 years, a Kali-kalpa. Cayce adds another dating for pole shifts and new Pole Stars using the Great Pyramid of Giza. On July 1, 1932, Edgar Cayce gave a reading that spoke of a change in the Pole Star of Earth.

He explained that the Great Pyramid of Giza represented the various ages we have been going through. He said, "At the correct time accurate imaginary lines can be drawn from the opening of the great Pyramid to the second star in the Great Dipper, called Polaris or the North Star." He must be using the word "Great" as an adjective of importance because Polaris is in the Little Dipper, but North Star is the *second* star in the constellation.

He said, "This indicates it is the system toward which the soul takes its flight after having completed its sojourn through this solar system. In October [of 1932] there will be seen the first variation in the position of the polar star in relation to the lines from the Great Pyramid. The dipper is gradually changing, and when this change becomes noticeable - as might be calculated from the Pyramid - there will be the beginning of the change in the races [he's speaking of *root* races not color races]. There will come a greater influx of souls from the Atlantean, Lemurian, La, Ur, or Da civilizations."

Let's examine the relationship of the entrance to the Great Pyramid and the Pole Stars. There are three Pole Stars for our little blue planet: Thuban, Polaris, and Vega. During the age of ancient Egypt, Thuban was the North Star, i.e., at midnight above the North Pole. Thuban was closest to the North Pole from 3942 BC until 1793 BC. Of course, today the North Star is Polaris; and Vega will be the North Star in the future. However, I could not get Vega to come into position until the year 10,000 AD. Cayce is obviously talking about a time much closer to the present. The only way for that to happen is a faster pole shift. Interestingly, if one draws an imaginary line from the entrance of the Great Pyramid on the Spring Equinox (about March 22-25) in 4000 BC, 2000 AD, and 10000 AD, it points directly to the northern star of each age: Thuban, Polaris, and Vega, respectively. Hermes, Ra, and all the others involved sure knew what they were doing when they built that magnificent monument.

Since Polaris indicates "the system towards which the soul takes flight," could the change to Vega indicate a new flight pattern for souls leaving this world, this dimension of life? Vega is a blue-white star and the fifth brightest star in the sky. It is in the constellation Lyra, the Harp or Lyre of the musician Orpheus. It was said that when Orpheus played this instrument, neither mortal nor god could turn away (Orpheus also introduced reincarnation into Greek mythology). Interestingly, Vega marks the approximate direction toward which our sun and all its planets are traveling through space.

Here's the hard news: In order to have shifted from Thuban as the Pole Star to Polaris, the Earth would have had to shift its northern axis pole about 26°, not a drastic shift. However, in order to shift from Polaris as the Pole Star to Vega, the Earth will have to shift its northern axis pole a whopping 51°! But, if it is done gradually over a very long period of time -- as Cayce seemed to indicate it would, then we should not be expecting a dramatic pole shift.

Pole shifts are not new to the Earth. Our geologists have evidence that magnetic pole shifts have occurred about every 100,000 years or so. A magnetic pole shift would cause some tremendous problems with communications and weather, but not necessarily a lot of physical destruction. However, during the magnetic shift we could assume that the Van Allen Belts that surround our planet would temporarily breakdown or disappear until a realignment of the new magnetic pattern was established. This could be very harmful to life on the planet. The Van Allen Belts are magnetic fields that surround the Earth, channeling incoming radiation from space toward our poles, keeping it from coming into our main living areas on the planet. The luminous bands of the Aurora Borealis (Northern Lights) and the Aurora Australis (Southern Lights) are the visual signs of these magnetic waves coming down through our atmosphere near our northern and southern poles. It is believed that as a magnetic shift began, the Belts would have to break up for a time, perhaps a few hours, a few days, a few months or a few years, until the new magnetic poles were established. Then, presumably the Belts would reestablish their magnetic field around the planet, channeling the incoming radiation to the new poles. During this period, the Earth would be exposed to increased levels of radiation. Perhaps this is the "fire" that so many prophecies speak of – the first cleansing having been by water inundation (the Great Flood); and the second is prophesied to be by fire, likely solar radiation.

If, on the other hand, the pole shift is not simply magnetic, but is a true *physical* changing of the poles -- in other words, the physical planet becomes unstable on its present axis, eventually rolls over and establishes a new axis – then there would very likely be destruction with the movement of the tectonic plates, shifting of the seas, and changes in weather patterns.

From Cayce's visions the pole shift means the present age is ending and a new one is beginning. Cayce said that during this new age we will regain the powers we had prior to becoming so encased in matter; and we will be able to use these powers to solve our material needs more easily. Of course, he warns that we had these powers during the time of Atlantis and we did not handle the powers well. Let's hope we've learned something over the past 12,000 years.

## 1998 - 2038: Cayce's Year of Great Events

The Cayce readings make six references to the year 1998. All six are significant statements. However, as you will see, each is in a different context. Three are in the context of the Ancient Atlantean and Egyptian period being karmically driven into play again during our lives, with the purposes, powers and souls that were involved then returning to life for another try. Without going into the entire Atlantis/Egypt story, I have tried to include enough of the readings' context to give you the true perspective of the readings. In two of the other three readings, a seeker who is familiar with Jacob Boehme's work is asking the sleeping Cayce a series of questions about the Aquarian Age when she also gets the 1998 date.

Here are the six references to 1998 with their respective reading numbers:

294-151: "Then began the laying out of the pyramid and the building of same. This had begun in those very mountains where they had taken refuge. It was not only built to remain as a place for receiving offers, just as those in the Temple Beauty where upon various altars an individual's innate self was offered, but to be the place of initiation of the initiates.

"The pyramid was formed according to the position of various stars around which this particular solar system circles – *going towards what?* Toward that same place to which the priest [Edgar Cayce was the reincarnation of the high priest "RaTa"] was banished – the constellation of Libra, or to Libya were these people sent. Is it not fitting then, that these people must return? As this priest [Edgar Cayce] may develop himself to be in that position to be a LIBERATOR of the world in its relationships to individuals in those periods to come; for he must enter again in that period, or in 1998.

"As the changes come about in the Earth, those things that were preserved were to later be made known in the minds of those peoples to come. The rise and fall of nations were to be depicted in this same temple which acted as an interpreter for that which had been, which is, and which is to be in the material plane."

There are many strange and curious statements in this reading. I particularly found the comment about "those things that were preserved were to later make known in the minds of those peoples to come." In other readings, Cayce clearly states that we are "those people to come" and that the images and concepts in the pyramids and other temples are to help us fully realize who we were, are, and what we are to be become. Let's continue with the 1998 readings:

378-14: "The apex of the pyramid (which has long since been removed by the sons of Heth [the sons of Noah's son Ham in Genesis 10:15]) was of metal. It was to be indestructible, being of copper, brass and gold with other alloys.

"Gizeh [sic] was to be the place of the initiates and their gaining understanding by personal application and the journeys through various activities in the earth. Then it was fitting that the placing of crown on the pyramid, this symbol of the record, was done by one who represented both the old and the new; one representing the Sons of the Law in Atlantis, Lemuria, Oz and Og. So, Hept-supht, he who keeps the record shut, was chosen as the one to seal that in the tomb.

"The old record in Gizeh is from the journey to the Pyrenees to the death of the Son of Man, as a man, and then to 1998."

This last sentence refers to the time-line in the Great Pyramid, which I outlined in a previous chapter of this book. But the reference to the Pyrenees is striking because it is also part of the Nostradamus End-Times material and the Divine Feminine's apparitions, many of which occurred in the Pyrenees Mountains. Continuing with the 1998 readings, we have this series of questions:

1602-3: "Q: Is the gradual restoration of phosphorus in man so he will talk back and forth with Cosmos, like the radio principle?

"A: This is gradually a development of which the awareness of the use of the spiritual consciousness may be a medium through which such may be done.

"Q: What does the restoration of phosphorus signify?

"A: The relationship of the individual to that awareness of the Universal Consciousness, which is the promise of all who have wholly put on Him. For as He has given, 'he that abideth wholly in me and I in him, to him will be made aware all things from the foundations of the world.' This is ALL there, in His words, in His promises to man [John 14 through 17]. Just as indicated in His exhortation upon the revelation activities of John, and as to what they meant in the affairs of man. That place, that awareness. And yet, when individuals will, even as John, become aware of being within the presence of Life itself, God Himself made manifest, how few accepted it?

"Q: What will the Aquarian Age mean to mankind as regards Physical, Mental and Spiritual development?

"A: These are as growths. In the center of the Piscean Age we had the entrance of "Emmanuel" or God among men, see? What did that mean? The same will be meant by the full consciousness of the ability to communicate with the Creative Forces, and the uses of same in material environs.

"This awareness in the age of Atlantis and Lemuria brought what? The destruction of man, and his beginning of the journey up through selfishness.

"Q: Why is the Aquarian Age described as the 'Age of the Lily?'

"A: The purity. Only the purity as it represents will be able to comprehend or understand that awareness that is before those who seek the way.

"Q: Can a date be given to indicate the beginning of the Aquarian Age?

"A: It laps over from one to another, as he holds to that which has been, which is -- as has been indicated, we will begin to understand fully in '98.

"Q: Three hundred years ago Jacob Boehme decreed Atlantis would rise again at this crisis time when we cross from this Piscean Era into the Aquarian. Is Atlantis rising now? Will it cause a sudden convolution and about what year?

"A: In 1998 we may find a great deal of the activities as have been wrought by the gradual changes that are coming about. These are at the periods when the cycle of the solar activity, or the years as related to the sun's passage through the various spheres of activity become paramount to the change between the Piscean and the Aquarian age. This is a *gradual*, not a cataclysmic activity in the experience of the earth in this period."

Ms. 1602 is an amazing seeker, and her questioning of the sleeping Cayce has brought us some important information. As we shall see, the End Times prophecies include many comments about our bodies being changed. Here Ms. 1602 gets Cayce to identify that phosphorus is rising in our bodies and will someday be sufficient for us to "become aware of being within the presence of Life itself, God Himself made manifest." She also gets Cayce to identify one of the primary qualities of this new era. Saying the last era was "God among men," Cayce says this coming era will be "the full consciousness of the ability to communicate with the Creative Forces, and the uses of same in material environs."

Continuing with the 1998 readings, we have a father hoping that he and his family can join with Cayce on his return during this great era:

2285-1: "Q: Will I, or any of my immediate family, reincarnate with Mr. Cayce in 1998?

"A: This is not to be given, or things of such a nature, but is to be determined by the desire, the need, the application of those who may desire to do so."

Finally, we have a reading that is truly remarkable for its clear dating of the return of the Messiah. I found it curious that Cayce chose that term to identify this coming Being. It seems to indicate a universalness to the coming, rather than the specific religion-connected term, Christ. Of course, even the Christ said he had flocks beyond the one he came to. Here's the reading, again referencing the Great Pyramid and the Xerxes material we discussed in the previous chapter:

5748-5: "In this same pyramid did the Great Initiate, the Master, take those last of the Brotherhood degrees with John, the forerunner of Him, at that place. As is indicated in that period where entrance is shown to be in that land that was set apart, as that promised to that peculiar peoples, as were rejected - as is shown in that portion when there is the turning back from the raising up of Xerxes as the deliverer from an unknown tongue or land, and again is there seen that this occurs in the entrance of the Messiah in this period - 1998."

Obviously, the year 1998 is a significant one from Edgar Cayce's perspective. Nostradamus viewed 1999 as a key marker. Frankly, these two seers were so close in their timing for a significant change that a one-year variation does not amount to much in my opinion.

If we add the Mayan's prophecy that the recent

age, which they called "the age of movement," ended in December of 2012, and Cayce's Great Pyramid timeline, which ends in 2038, then clearly the years from 1998 through to 2038 are when much of this prophesied change is to occur.

## Cayce & the End Times

As we have seen, the Cayce readings contain many references to the biblical prophecies about the End Times. Perhaps the most amazing one is his bold statement that "the time, times and half-times" spoken of in the prophet Daniel's vision are over! Clearly this means that the End Time is upon us. There can be no other interpretation of such a statement. In fact, the Edgar Cayce readings repeatedly state that "the time, times and half-times" are over.

## The Armageddon

The end of the time, times and halftimes means that a great battle is about to take place between the forces of the light and good and the forces of the darkness and evil. So, for Cayce, the end of the time, times and halftimes is the beginning of the last great battle of Armageddon. After which a thousand years of peace reign with "Satan bound." You may recall how Halaiel referenced this period in his earth-change reading:

3976-15: "And those that in the inmost recesses of theirselves awaken to the spiritual truths that are to be given, and those places that have acted in the capacity of teachers among men, the rottenness of those that have ministered in places will be brought to light, and turmoils and strifes shall enter. And, as there is the wavering of those that would enter as emissaries, as teachers, from the throne of life, the throne of light, the throne of immortality, and wage war in the air with those of darkness, *then know ye the Armageddon is at hand*. For with the great numbers of the gathering of the hosts of those that have hindered and would make stumblingblocks for man and his weaknesses, *they shall wage war with the spirits of light that come into the earth for this awakening;* that have been and are being called by those of the sons of men into the service of the living God. For He, as ye have been told, is not the God of the dead, not the God of those that have forsaken Him, but those that love His coming, that love His associations among men - the God of the LIVING, the God of Life! For, He IS Life."

There are two more references to the Armageddon in the Cayce readings. One relates to the Great Pyramid in Giza and the other to the spirituality of the American people.

5748-6: "Q: If the Armageddon is foretold in the Great Pyramid, please give a description of it and the date of its beginning and ending.

"A: Not in what is left there. It will be as a thousand years, with the fighting in the air, and - as has been - between those returning to and those leaving the earth."

This certainly fits with the previous reading in which Halaliel describes Armageddon as a battle between "those that would enter as emissaries, as teachers, from the throne of life, the throne of light, the throne of immortality, and wage war in the air with those of darkness." It is also important to note that the Armageddon is to last a thousand years. Hopefully, the end of this war is near, and the thousand years of peace will begin soon.

900-272, given in October of 1926: "These are rather the conditions as may be expected: The spirituality of the American people will be the criterion of that as is to become the world's forces. As has been given in that of the peace table [Versailles, 1919, ending WW I], there sat the Master in the American people, with the brotherhood of the world accepted - war was at an end. Without same [spirituality and the brotherhood of the world] there will again come the Armageddon [WW II?], and in same there will be seen that the Christian forces will AGAIN move westward."

The USA is a survivor of the hot and cold wars of the 1900s. Is our spirituality intact? Do we still hold to the brotherhood of the world?

### A Noah-like Time

There is a fascinating reading for a woman who was on Noah's ark. But in the reading Cayce gives some further insights into the coming changes and their relationship to the changes that occurred during Noah's time. You'll recall, even Jesus references Noah's time on the Mount of Olives. The reading begins with Cayce's mind looking over this woman's "Book of Life," her records on the skein of time and space:

3653-1: "What an unusual record - and one of those who might be termed as physically 'the mothers of the world!' Because the entity was one of those in Noah's ark.

"The entity has appeared when there were new revelations to be given. And again it appears when there are new revelations to be made.

"May the entity so conduct its mind, its body and its purposes, then, as to be a channel through which such messages may come that are needed for the awakenings in the minds of men as to the necessity for returning to the search for their relationship with the Creative Forces or God.

"For as has been given from the beginning, the deluge [Noah's flood] was not a myth (as many would have you believe) but a period when man had so belittled himself with the cares of the world, with the deceitfulness of his own knowledge and power, as to require that there be a return to his dependence wholly - physically and mentally - upon the Creative Forces.

"Will this entity see such again occur in the earth? Will it be among those who may be given directions as to how, where, the elect may be preserved for the replenishing again of the earth?

"Remember, not by water - for it is the mother of life in the earth - but rather by the elements, fire."

This is a disturbing reading. It seems to be saying that there will be a new destruction, like the one that occurred during Noah's period, yet this time it will be by fire not water. And it also seems to be saying that the destruction will be of such a magnitude that we'll be "given directions as to how, where, the elect may be preserved for the replenishing again of the earth!"

I know many of us hate these doom prophecies. They are so depressing that it appears impossible to live our daily lives with them hanging over our heads. All I can trust in – with my own wife, children and hopes for this life – is Jesus' teaching that with God *all things are possible*. It's also important to realize that this reading does clearly indicate that life will go on, as it did after Noah.

As I've mentioned previously, the fire mentioned in this reading could possibly come from the increase in radiation as the Van Allen Belts break down. This would be "like a fire" and would affect the whole Earth.

On the whole, the Cayce readings are positive and encouraging about the future and its potential. They do predict major changes during this next period. Here is a list of the changes predicted in the Cayce readings.

## Reincarnation & Soul Groups

As you know, Edgar Cayce taught that reincarnation was occurring. He gave many readings for people in which he explained that current situations in their lives were due to past activities of their inner soul, even if the outer person did not remember or know about them. He stated that the soul had karma, things to meet in this life that were caused by actions in past lives. He also taught that souls travel in what he called, soul groups. Since many of his predictions about wars dealt with the karma of these soul groups, let's look at what he said about the tensions between the Middle Eastern and Western soul groups. The event of September 11, 2001, in which terrorists from the Middle East attacked the World Trade Center and the U.S. Pentagon, are, according to Cayce, not just current events, but have past motivations and karma behind them. Amazingly, he refers to the Crusades as the beginning of the tensions between Middle Eastern and Western people's soul groups. The Crusades occurred from 1095 to 1291.

In a fascinating support of Cayce's perspective, Osama bin Laden compared himself to *Salah al-Din*, better known in the Western world as *Saladin*, the Muslim military leader who recaptured the Holy Land from the Christian Crusaders in 1187 A.D. and defeated Richard the Lion-Heart. From that time until 1917, the Holy Land, including Palestine and Jerusalem, has been held by Moslems (with only two very brief periods of Christian rule). For Arab Muslims, Saladin is the symbol of Moslem greatness against Christian dominance. He was the victorious leader who overthrew the Christians and ended the Crusades. Saladin's massive Citadel still stands in Cairo, Egypt, today.

Jerusalem has been in Muslim hands since 638 A.D. However, the earlier Muslim rulers allowed Christian pilgrims to come and go. They worked cooperatively with Byzantine Christians (Eastern Orthodox), who considered themselves to be the guardians of the Christian faith and the Holy Land. The Byzantines were not religious bigots, allowing a mosque to be built in their capital, Constantinople, and received emissaries from Muslim courts, honoring them and showing respect for their ways and beliefs. Yet, the Muslim Seljuk

Turks changed all of that when they overthrew the more moderate Muslim leadership and took control of the Holy City in 1071. The Crusades began in 1095, when Pope Urban II gave a speech in France, with an appeal for the people to rise up against the Muslim Seljuk Turks who had stopped Christian pilgrimages to the Holy Lands.

According to St. Augustine, the objective of a just war was vindication of justice, meaning the defense of a people's life and property. But this was a new type of war, a war for the defense of the faith – a Holy War. The code of the just war called for good faith with the enemy, regard for non-combatants, respect for hostages and prisoners. Yet, all such restraints were abandoned in dealing with the "infidel." In a fascinating twist of history, the warrant for this new view of warfare was found in the biblical account of the conquest of Canaan by Joshua (Joshua 1:1-4), dating back to 1451 B.C. The rallying cry among the Crusaders was *Deus vult!* ("God wills it"). This same warrant from God to Joshua is often used by the current rulers of the Holy City, the Jews, who feel that God gave this land to them, and it is their divine right to take it from those who hold it.

Though the Byzantines supported the intent of the Holy War, they were surprised and upset that the northern Christian Crusaders (French-Norman, German, and English), who previously held to strict rules of war and military conduct, dropped these principles when fighting against the Muslims, killing combatants and non-combatants alike (civilians, women and children), razing cities and plundering not only Moslem cities, but even attempting to capture Durazzo from the Byzantine Christians for no better reason than to gain the wealth of the city for their Holy War. The brutality and crude zeal of the northern Crusaders left many, including some Crusaders, feeling badly about this war. Jerusalem fell to the Crusaders in 1099. Records tell of how "the Crusaders waded to their ankles in the blood of the infidel, then proceeded to the Church of the Holy Sepulcher, singing in jubilation that Christ had conquered."

In reaction to the Crusades, the Muslims began a series of counterattacks, but none succeeded until Saladin.

Saladin was born of Kurdish parents. His full name means, "Righteous of the Faith, Joseph, son of Job." In his youth he studied religious concepts more than military ones. But he eventually joined the staff of the armies and participated in three expeditions into Egypt to prevent it from falling into French Christian hands. In 1161, at the age of 31, Saladin was appointed commander of the Syrian troops and vizier of Egypt. He countered the Shiite Moslem movement and reestablished Sunnism in Egypt (bin Laden is a Sunni Muslim as well). He moved out of Egypt with a small but highly disciplined army, uniting the Muslims of Syria, Mesopotamia, and Palestine. Like bin Laden, Saladin had an intense sense of *jihad*, Holy War. Eventually, this led to his reconquering the Holy Land from the Crusaders. In stark contrast to the city's conquests by the Christians, when blood flowed freely during the barbaric slaughter of its inhabitants, the Muslim reconquest was marked by the civilized good faith and courteous behavior of Saladin and his troops. In October 1192, Richard the Lion-Heart set sail for England, and the Crusades were virtually over. Five months later, on March 4, 1193, Saladin died, with not enough money to buy the land for his grave. But he was, and remains, one of the greatest heroes of Moslem history.

Was Osama bin Laden the reincarnation of Saladin? Whether he was or not, he was driven to counter the growing Christian presence in his world (including U.S. airbases) and break any alliances with Israel.

Over the many years that Edgar Cayce read the Akashic Records, he gave past-life readings for 102 souls who had incarnated during the times of the original Holy Wars between Moslems and Christians, giving readings for both Christians and Moslems who lived in those times. In some of his readings, he referred to the Crusaders as "zealous ones" (355-1) who came to take back the Holy City from perceived heathens, but found in their contacts with the Moslems that they had a brotherly love and showed it to many Crusaders who were captured or injured and came under their care. They also learned that these "infidels" had a science and hygiene that was in many respects superior to that of the Crusaders. However, Cayce also noted how dramatically different was the loving expression of the Moslems in those days from the Moslems today (1135-1). Yet, Cayce never wavered from his principle of oneness and brotherhood of all peoples: "For whether they be Greek, Parthenian, Jew or Gentile - whether they be of Mohammed, Confucius, or even Shinto or On or Mu - the Lord, thy God, is ONE! For all force, all power that is manifested in thyself, is of the ONE source" (1494-1). In another he said, "Let that rather be thy watchword, 'I am my brother's keeper.' Who is thy brother? Whoever, wherever he is, that bears the imprint of the Maker in the earth, be he black, white, gray or grizzled, be he young, be he Hottentot, or on the throne or in the president's chair. All that are in the earth today are thy brothers. Those that have gradually forgotten God entirely have been eliminated, and there has come - now - and will come at the close of this next year - the period when there will be no part of the globe where man has not had the opportunity to hear, 'The Lord He is God.' And, as has been indicated, *when this period has been accomplished, then the new era, the new age, is to begin.* Will ye have a part of it, or will ye let it pass by and be merely a hanger-on, or one upon whom your brother - the Lord, thy Christ - may depend?" (2780-3) My italics.

Cayce also cautioned against war out of anger or revenge. He told one Crusader, "Yet in those periods the entity learned much: that they who fight, they who war against their brethren find themselves warring as against the spirit of truth. For that as is sown in anger, that as is sown in dread, must be reaped in turmoil and in strife" (1226-1).

### Edgar Cayce's Prophecies End *Positively!*

Because so much of Cayce's material is about earthquakes, volcanoes, and wars, he is often considered one of the prophets of doom. But, he clearly states that all of these changes are necessary in order to clean up unfinished business or karma, both within individual souls and among soul groups. The new age that follows these changes is a wonderful age of enlightenment, love, and cooperation. He repeats the statement in the Revelation that during this future age "Satan will be bound," meaning that all evil will be in check. But it cannot be entered until all the negative, evil influences within us are cleansed. This is a concept that we saw in the prophecies of the Virgin Mary, in which she too states that there will be a "chastisement." It is in the biblical prophecies: "Whom God loves, he chastens, everyone." But if Cayce is correct, *the way* to this new era of banished evil and illuminating love and light is a challenging one.

**Edgar Cayce**

Edgar Cayce's last name is the French version of the English name *Casey*, and is pronounced, *kay-see*.

**Other Books by John Van Auken**

- *Passage in Consciousness: A Guide to Expanding Our Minds and Raising the Life Forces in Our Bodies through Deep Meditation*
- *Reincarnation & Karma: Our Soul's Past-Life Influences*
- *From Karma to Grace: The Power of the Fruits of the Spirit*
- *Edgar Cayce on the Spiritual Forces Within Us*
- *Angels, Fairies, Dark Forces, and the Elements: With the Edgar Cayce Perspective on the Supernatural World*
- *Edgar Cayce on Health, Healing, and Rejuvenation*
- *Edgar Cayce on the Mysterious Essenes: Lessons from Our Sacred Past*
- *2038: Great Pyramid Timeline Prophecy*
- *Edgar Cayce's Amazing Interpretation of The Revelation*
- *Hidden Teachings of Jesus*
- *A Broader View of Jesus Christ*
- *Edgar Cayce and the Kabbalah: A Resource for Soulful Living*
- *Ancient Egyptian Visions of Our Soul Life*
- *Mayan Toltec Aztec Visions of Our Soul Life*

All Titles and more are available on Amazon.com

John Van Auken
*Living in the Light Newsletter*
P.O. Box 4942
Virginia Beach, VA 23454
JohnVanAuken.com

Made in the USA
Middletown, DE
16 February 2020